Broken
to
Unbreakable

12 STEPS TO AN UNBREAKABLE
MIND, BODY & SPIRIT

KRISSY REGAN
THE WELLNESS POET

First published by Ultimate World Publishing 2020
Copyright © 2020 Krissy Regan

ISBN

Paperback - 978-1-922372-24-6
Ebook - 978-1-922372-25-3

Cover design: Ultimate World Publishing
Layout and typesetting: Ultimate World Publishing
Editor: Felicity Frankish

Ultimate World Publishing
Diamond Creek,
Victoria Australia 3089
www.writeabook.com.au

"Krissy's journey to wellness is inspirational and her poetry is very moving. She communicates ideas, thoughts and emotions so fluently, it will leave you wanting more!"

Louise Vangestel, Sydney, Australia

"With her insightful writing and poetry on wellbeing, Krissy gives a voice to others. She expresses with honesty and skill, the thoughts, emotions and experiences which many find relatable. I wish her every success with this book."

Liezel Gordon,
Clinical Psychologist, Townsville, Australia

"Krissy combines a wealth of experience in leadership, project management, client handling and team development. Her training programs are unique, due to her ability to translate complex messages in an engaging, fun and memorable way. Krissy has created bespoke training programs for both our internal and external clients for the past three years and it's always a pleasure to attend her sessions."

Yael Cole-Slagter,
Director of Operations, SQR group, London

"Wow, what a difference four weeks can make and have such a positive impact on your life! I have learnt so much in Krissy's program, new skills, lots of great new powerful knowledge and much more. I have been living in my comfort zone for so long now. I feel I can now break free from my 'Safe Place' and move beyond that into my Growth and Learning Zones, which was my biggest aha moment of all. I now understand the importance of 'Filling my Cup' first, because at the end of the day if a mum's cup is full, everyone in the family will benefit. I'm very excited to start setting goals, short term and long term, and strive to achieve them along my life journey."

Haley Hopkins, Townsville, Australia

Dedication

This book is dedicated to my two wonderful daughters for whom I've suffered so much, but feel so much joy and pride when I look at them. My hope is that they grow up to be strong, independent, creative, resilient, kind, innovative, compassionate and just a little bit selfish, when it comes to taking care of themselves.

When my eldest daughter was four, she told me she would like to be a Fairy Godmother when she grows up, so she can make all the children's wishes come true in the world. This is the most beautiful thing I have ever heard and she amazes me every day with her insights and wisdom.

This book is also a gentle reminder for me of her twin who did not make it, but who will never be forgotten. I know that in her sacrifice, another miracle was possible.

I'm grateful for my struggles to become a mum, so I can now appreciate these moments of sheer joy and genuine wonder.

Contents

Introduction

This is a book about a journey to find a version of yourself that is new, different and stronger than you are right now, because somewhere along the line you got stuck, trapped and maybe a little broken under the weight of yourself. You may have not even noticed this weight creep up on you, as it happened gradually over time. As you get older it's necessary to shed the weight of expectations before they destroy you. The weight of our expectations plays a large part in how we live our life.

The expectations I am referring to include:

- Are you healthy?
- Are you successful at work?
- Do you have enough money?
- Are you a good person, parent, friend, colleague, boss?
- Have you lived up to your potential?
- Are you disappointing those closest to you?
- Have you let yourself down?

- Have you failed to conceive and follow the time line you set for yourself as a teenager?
- Have you had a physical, emotional or mental breakdown?
- Have you fallen out with people you care about?
- Have you lost your sense of self while role-playing wife, mum, dad, partner, husband, martyr?
- Have you abused your mind and body so much that it can no longer support you?
- Did you choose a path that is no longer serving you?
- Did you make some decisions that cost you a lot?
- Did you go against your family's wishes and try to choose your own destiny?
- Are you a giver – giving, giving and giving and not receiving?
- Have you bitten off more than you can chew, and instead of spitting it out, you would rather choke than give up?
- Do you care anymore?

These are big questions. Before you start worrying about the answers, let me say this: these expectations manifest in so many ways and it's very easy to get trapped in your expectations and then to look back after a decade or two and realise that you've limited yourself and the version of you in the mirror is the worst version of yourself.

When that realisation hits, watch out. You may fall to the floor and give up, thinking it's already too late. Or, you will decide to rebuild, and both take a lot of energy – remember as much energy is needed to give up as to rebuild. Choosing which one to embrace in that moment is up to you, but giving up is more expensive than rebuilding. Often, we don't decide to change until it's almost too late. This could be when:

- We have a health scare.
- We lose someone close to us.
- We lose our job.

And pretty soon all that is familiar and comfortable becomes untangled, including what we know and believe.

So, how do we go about repairing ourselves and project managing ourselves to become unbreakable? In my opinion, the most basic form of project management (i.e. rebuilding or rebooting yourself) is to start at the end and work backwards. Yes, start at the end of your life and determine how you want to be living and what you want to be doing when you are 90, 80, 70, 60, 50, 40 and so on. Being clear about the future will help you determine the best version of yourself in the present. You will then go on to live as you wish in those later years.

Let's forget chronological age for a moment, because we all have the power to positively and negatively influence our biological age. Do you want your biological age to be positive to your chronological age, or do you want to be in the negative? Ask yourself that big question and then hit STOP! Mull on it for a few days. Let it stew and fester and think about all the most important people in your life and then decide if you want to leave the park brake on, (negative biological age) or take it off (positive biological age).

Here's a quick example of what I'm talking about:

When my childhood friend was 45 years old he was involved in a serious accident. Thankfully he recovered, but was suffering from back pain, so he thought he would visit a chiropractor. Considering he had just sustained a lot of internal injuries in his accident, he decided to have an X-ray on his back to check if things were okay. What he was told frightened him. His spine had degenerated and was the equivalent to a spine of a 70-year-old. He hit STOP! He has three young children, was 45 years old and was told his back is 30 years older than he is.

This is not just common in society today, it is endemic. But the great news is, we are never too old to positively influence our health and wellbeing, and you can start right now. We are also never too old to learn the information we need to make the changes that are right for us. All the information that can help you create an unbreakable mind, body and spirit is out there, free to consume at your pace. However, I promise you that once you engage with content that enables you to live a happy, healthier, longer life, you will soak it up like gravy on white bread.

According to the World Health Organization, stress is the number one killer of people today – it's an epidemic. What causes us the most stress? Expectations, fear, busy schedules, negative thoughts, money worries, break-ups, breakdowns and our failing health or that of our loved ones.

Among many subjects covered in this book, we will look closely at the impacts of stress. How it affects our entire body physiologically, energetically and mentally. Your expectations may take a beating as well, because we are going to consider the impacts of expectations and the excuses we make for ourselves.

Very often, we hand over responsibility for ourselves to others, to fix, heal, repair, remodel, make new, shape and look nice. What I'm here to tell you, is that when you release responsibility for yourself to others, you hand over your power. Unless you are an excellent project manager, the you that you hoped for, will only ever be the you they have the time or inclination to give you. This is also the most expensive option. The other option, and all the steps in this book, are FREE!

Think for a moment about **accountability** – it is not only about being responsible for what you do, but also being able to give a satisfactory reason for why.

Starting this moment, look in the mirror and say to yourself:

"I'm the only person responsible for me!"

The power in this statement is that you take total accountability for your health and wellbeing.

I'm conscious that at the time of finalising this book, we are in the early stages of the Coronavirus pandemic and the long-term implications of this may not be understood for a very long time. Many people will suffer physically and financially and I pray for everyone affected. I call myself a Wellness Warrior, wanting to spread a message of health and wellness like a virus. I still believe that we can do this and help minimise the impact of illness and diseases. Taking accountability for our own health is the first step.

Of course, you can employ professional support along the way to help guide you, and if needed, fix some of the broken bits. But long term, you need to become the CEO and operations director of self!

Sensible

Expectations

Last

Forever

My advice is do not wait until it's too late to create the future you would like. We spend so much of our life waiting for things to happen and waiting for the future to arrive, we get in our own way. How can we make our current life as joyful, healthy and fun as possible?

We can stop mulling, take full responsibility and get on with this plan that is going to lay some new foundations to help build the strongest version of you right now and in the long term.

Foundations do take time to lay and they need to be solid before you can build on them. The best-preserved roads in the world are those laid by the Romans over 2,000 years ago. These days the materials we use to make roads don't last more than a few years, if we are lucky. I want to make your foundations strong, so no matter how many people stomp all over them they are unbreakable, durable but flexible, capable of weathering any storm and are a super highway into your future.

To lay this forever road we may need to strip back the crumbly surface of your life and dig deep into your feelings, thinking and beliefs. The hardest part of this process is even knowing where to begin. Where do you start when you are not sure if anything is even wrong with you?

> *"Am I broken? Is something wrong with me? I'm just like everybody else. Hardworking, dedicated, independent, resilient, reliable. I'm not perfect, but I am not a total mess. I've had my share of trauma and heartbreak and I've survived, and by some standards, thrived, in spite of them."*

Thriving – now there is a word that has become very trendy lately. Not only do I want you to thrive, I want you to radiate health, love, joy, compassion and conviction.

Here's my story:

I wasn't even sure if I was broken, but something wasn't right. I was so caught up in being busy, meeting expectations and getting things done. I was too busy to look after myself, according to my inner voice. However, my body started shutting down after decades of neglect and I started to feel broken.

My brokenness was not one single event, but an accumulation of events over a lifetime that were unacknowledged and misunderstood even by myself. I confess, it caught me by surprise, as it may with many high-functioning women who are task orientated and whose values include accountability, helping and not letting people down.

In my mid 40s I hit STOP! I recognised that my biological age was much older than my actual age and I was suffering with many health conditions, including back pain, hip pain, foot pain, chronic abnormal liver function, adrenal fatigue, breast cysts, headaches, insomnia, mood swings, anxiety, mild depression and I was obese, according to my BMI (Body Mass Index: 18.5–24.9 normal, 25–29.9 overweight, over 30 obese).

Obese is not a nice word and not easy to swallow when you have generally been fairly active at certain periods in your life. Or like me, you consider yourself a relatively healthy size 14–16 and all your nice clothes are in that sizing!

My mindset and my conditions, listed above, kept me trapped in what was a whole series of unhealthy choices and bad habits. When I started to take responsibility for my health and wellbeing, I realised how unkind I was to my body and I had largely ignored my mental and spiritual health and I needed to take action.

I knew it was not going to be easy, it was going to get pretty uncomfortable, but I did not want to spend the next few decades visiting the hospital and waiting in a doctor's office to be given bad news! So, I took off my park brake, I got out of my way and I laid a new foundation. It's this foundation I want to share with you, so that your life can be everything that you deserve in the most positive way. Come with me and embrace the effects of living life as you could, not as you would have.

By the way, my end date is 2083 (107 years of age) or thereabouts. Why? Because I had my children late and I want to be a grandmother. So, in my 90s I want to bounce babies on my knees, get invited to parties and drink champagne. In my 80s I want to travel the world, meet brilliant people and share stories. In my 70s I want to support my children as they figure out their own lives (the tumultuous 30s) and in my 50s and 60s I will have teenage girls, so I need to be fit and healthy – mentally, emotionally and physically.

Before we go deeply into the 12 Steps there are two important facts you need to know:

1. It takes between 18–60 days to form new habits. The funny thing about habits is that, unless you have a new healthy habit to replace the bad habit, you will never fully move it on out of your life. It will just be something that you avoid. Replacing bad habits with good habits ensures the bad ones move on out, because there is no space for them in your life any longer.

2. The cells of our body are constantly dying and regenerating and every 12–18 months many of our cells have regenerated. Can you imagine that in 12–18 months you have a relatively new body that you have shaped, created and future proofed, which enables you not only to live well now, but live well for longer.

There is no doubt that technology simplifies and speeds up life and allows us to learn and track our progress from the comfort of our sofa. We can all be enticed into a 7-day detox, 30 days to lose weight, 12 weeks to run 5kms, or an online coaching course where we never get to fully interact with any real people. These programs can be helpful to certain types of people, who may have the ability to maintain any gains they've made and embed them as part of new healthy habits long term. But what about those people that finish the challenge and revert to exactly how they were before?

We know it takes commitment and time to embrace and embed new habits, but how long does it take to realistically create a whole new you? How long does it take to rebuild yourself after years of bad habits, burnout, sustained stress, pain and suffering? It can take years for some people, but in this book, you will learn how to do it in one year.

Why is it one year? The 12 Steps in this plan are each 30 days to allow you to build those new and healthy habits into your daily routine. You will devote 30 days to each step, which includes realistic activities that sort, declutter, destress, motivate, help you learn, allow you to create, think and grow and in the process you will become fitter, healthier and happier.

The 12 Steps can follow the calendar months of the year, with a monthly theme aimed at creating introspection, reflection and action in order to create a shift from where you are now to where you want to go. But remember, in order to know where you want to go you have to spend some time considering this. That is why the first step in this journey is the most important!

You will need to set an intention that you will spend the best part of 30 days practising each step, in order to understand your habits and excuses, create new habits and embrace the changes to carry them forward as part of your new foundation.

By the time you reach Step 12 (in 12 months), you will be habitually and automatically doing all 11 previous steps as part of your life. Your foundations will be strong, you will have greater clarity of purpose, you will shed weight (mentally, physically and emotionally) and you will have a strong drive to continue this well into your end goal (your end date to be decided – in my case 2083).

You can of course start this process at any time, as long as you set an intention to follow each step for 30 days. My own personal journey followed the calendar months of the year.

Step	Activity	Month
1	Journaling	January
2	Filing	February
3	Mindfulness	March
4	Appreciation	April
5	Meditation	May
6	Joy	June
7	Jogging	July
8	Adventure	August
9	Socialising	September
10	Open	October
11	New	November
12	Devoted	December

"Is that it?" I can hear you thinking, *"There is no way I'm jogging for 30 days in July!"*

Just hold on a second: open mind and open heart is ground rule number one. I will guide you through these steps – the whys, the hows and the whens, and you won't have to think about them too much. Once you set an intention to really take action to meet your best future self, you will certainly not have any trouble getting through this. I'm also a realist, so if these steps raise a strong objection within you, I will suggest a work-a-round or two that will keep you moving forward, but not make you feel like a failure just by looking at this list of activities.

I'm inspired and humbled every day by ordinary people doing ordinary things and making a difference to a small number of people within their circle of influence. I've met and worked with famous people. Did they inspire me to want to become them? Absolutely not... Do I hope this book will inspire you to be the best version of yourself? Absolfreakinlootely! Do I want to go soul to soul with Oprah on Super Soul Sunday – hell yes!

So, are you ready to go on a journey with an open mind and an open heart and rebuild your mind, body and spirit?

"Peace begins when expectation ends."
Sri Chinmoy

"A life that is burdened with expectations is a heavy life. Its fruit is sorrow and disappointment."
Douglas Adams

STEP 1

Journaling

Is journaling a fad? I guess in some circles it might be considered so, but I believe it's an essential foundation for understanding yourself. As I mentioned in the introduction, in most cases quick fixes don't work.

A journal is not a diary where you write down things like, "Today I went for a walk and fed my dog". Although, if you want to put that in your journal, then do so.

For me, it started with wanting to write down some realisations I had about myself after reading Brené Brown's book, *The Gifts of Imperfection*. Not because I thought I was a perfectionist who needed help, but because the book shone a light on many of the weakest aspects of my character, let's call them growth opportunities.

I started writing down some aha moments as they came to me whilst reading the book. Then somehow, this little notebook took on a life of its own where I found myself writing down my most intimate secrets, thoughts and ideas. I started to understand that journaling was a window into the soul – our unspoken truths and the things we can't and won't say out loud to ourselves.

Here's a snapshot of what's in mine.

My own insights and my reactions to them:

- I am resilient and adaptable, I cope well with change.
- I practise/use numbing behaviours (to avoid my emotions), like alcohol, shopping and talking about others behind their back!
  - ➢ *"I do love shopping, but what a waste of energy to talk about others in a negative way!"*
- I am a caretaker.
- I avoid being seen as vulnerable and I do not process or feel my feelings.
  - ➢ *"I'm a tough cookie, according to most!"*

- I need to lean into discomfort, as true growth can only occur when we are outside of our comfort zone.
  - ➢ *"Crap, that sounds painful!"*
- Squandering your gifts brings you distress.
  - ➢ *"This was a huge one for me and rekindled my love of writing and poetry and TheWellnessPoet.com was born."*
- Be slow to respond and quick to think, not the other way around!
  - ➢ *"God, I'd f-d that up for a very long time..."*
- I am over-functioning: I like to advise, rescue, takeover, micromanage and I don't look inward often enough.
  - ➢ *"I guess that is what my old bosses had tried to tell me..."*
- I've lived much of the last decade in a state of constant stress (flight or fight).
  - ➢ *"Ah, so that's what might have caused my adrenal fatigue!"*
- I've not taken care of myself, physically, spiritually, emotionally or mentally.
  - ➢ *"I was too busy making money, making shit happen, making babies, making myself look good on the outside!"*
- I'm suffering with anxiety and I catastrophise situations, living in a constant state of worst-case scenario thinking.
  - ➢ *"I'm brilliant at catastrophising most situations in my head, it has kept me safe but is also killing me!"*
- I have an innate distrust of people who say they love me, who then may hurt me or let me down.
  - ➢ *"Hmm, let's just sit with that for a moment!"*
- I don't allow myself to be joyful or get too excited about anything.
  - ➢ *"No way, because in any moment something can be taken away from you!"*
- My relationship with words like anger, hurt, compassion, judgement and kindness is superficial and I do not respect the true meaning of them.
  - ➢ *"Uh oh, I may need therapy!"*

And BOOM! There it was… It didn't take too many nights of journaling for the reality of my emotional and mental state to be highlighted in ink right there in front of me. I thought: holy crap, what am I going to do about this? I had absolutely no idea, but realised I was free to figure it out as best as I could without pressure, expectations, judgement or fear.

Seeing my wisdom and insights written down like that sparked my curiosity and led me to read, research and contemplate them in order to acknowledge the importance of them, or to figure out what I wanted to do about them.

It might help here to explain how I found the worst version of myself in the mirror!

I had spent 15 years living abroad, working hard and playing hard, and then when I decided to try for a family, it didn't happen. For eight long years it did not happen and after several visits to several doctors and some minor procedures, I made the decision to try for children with the help of science. It's not an easy decision, and if you have an aversion to needles and blood tests then IVF is not going to sit well with you. It's freakin' hard work, it's expensive and at times people are just down right unkind and uncompassionate. If you are on the other side of the world from your family and close friends, then you really feel very lonely when you embark on something as emotionally draining as fertility treatment.

The other branch to this is that working hard had become my escape and I found myself sitting for 10–12 hours a day at my desk churning out spreadsheets and PowerPoint presentations, instead of churning off calories on a treadmill. I made many excuses not to take up organised activities, and as the years rolled on my butt got bigger, but so did my bank account so I was able to rationalise the cost.

This was in stark contrast to my teens and 20s when I was heavily involved in sport and had represented Australia at three World Championships and gained a degree in Exercise Science and Sports Management. Somewhere along the way, the healthy, happy, fun young woman became a serious, determined 30-something without much emphasis on fun or health.

It's hard to reconcile the path we choose in life or how we end up somewhere far from where we started. The interesting thing about journaling is that it can help you look back at your path and the diversions you have taken. If you are serious about understanding where you have come from, and where you want to go, you can use this information to help you gain some perspective, and plot a new course.

One interesting insight into my life came when I realised that as a child I was praised when I did chores. I liked being praised for helping, so I attached being 'helpful' to my self-worth and associated my value to how much I could help others. This was quite a revelation for me, as I do get a lot of satisfaction out of helping people, but I also did not have any boundaries. I often felt used and abused and that my generosity was not reciprocated and I was taken for granted.

Boundaries are hard to establish if you are unclear about your own values or ensuring your needs are met. Women are often guilty of neglecting their own needs for others, particularly if you happen to be a people pleaser or derive pleasure from helping others. If you are this way inclined before you have children, then you may only get worse once you do have them.

So, in order to figure out what was important to me, I needed to understand my own personal values. It can be hard to pinpoint a set of personal values, but after a bit of mulling I came up with the following list.

What are my values?

- Integrity.
- Helping.
- Not letting people down.
- Accountability.

Once I wrote down my values, I was clear about what behaviours in myself and others were unacceptable and why things pushed my buttons. For example, if someone repeatedly lets me down, or is not accountable, I feel very hurt, angry and resentful. Over the years I have worked with people who had low integrity and this had messed heavily with my conscience. Because they were paying me, I could not tell them they were big A-holes.

Here's the thing about values – when you are doing things or living contrary to your values, it affects you physically as well as emotionally and mentally. Anguish, hurt and illness can be traced to the abuse of our personal values.

Writing down your values is a great contract for yourself and you can then practise role modelling your values with your family and in your interactions with others. My relationship with some of my values had become quite superficial, as I had forgotten to honour my own values, which left me feeling drained, sick and quite fed up.

Your own personal values may not be the same as mine or even your partner's (if you have one), and that is OK, because there are literally hundreds of virtues that we take on as our personal values. Even if we do share the same values, it's very possible that you may not see them in the same way as I do, and therefore, we will have different ideas about how we practise helping or accountability.

It's much easier to explain your grievances or hurts to others when you link them to your values. You can explain how that person can make you feel according to your values. If the person's behaviour is completely unacceptable to your values, then it's a sure sign that the relationship is not healthy and you may need to step away from that person. Or in my case, reconcile why particular people had affected me so deeply throughout my life, whilst others were unimportant.

Kerry Spina, published a great book on virtues called:
The Little Book of Harmony.
www.kidsinharmony.com.au/little-book-harmony/

If you've never considered your values before, or those of your children and loved ones, it's worth checking out this book and taking some time to really explore your values and the behaviours you wish to see linked to them. Then you can truly hold yourself and others accountable and show up for people in the right way. This will bring you more personal accountability and fulfilment.

Journaling is personal and the idea for this book, and the 12 Steps that you are now following were written down in my journal in January 2019. It was then that I wrote my first poem in five years. The poems I had written prior to this were to honour people and occasions including births, deaths and marriages, and it dawned on me that writing poems was a good way of asking the questions and not trying to determine the answer. The answer would show up in whatever form it needed to, when I needed it.

In my journal I wrote down all the feelings I didn't want to fuel with energy any longer. Those that were not serving me and playing on a constant loop in my head. The old hurts, the old wrongs and the old pain bodies. If you want to know about pain bodies, Eckhart Tolle writes about it in his books *The Power of Now* and *A New Earth*.

I started writing down the feelings I did not want to dwell on any longer and I thought I would just keep going until I filled up one page and then stop that activity. The reality was quite different, because once I got to the bottom of that page, the flood gates were open and I filled two more pages.

That's a lot of baggage and a lot of unprocessed emotions. No wonder I was suffering with some anxiety and distrust for people.

To counterbalance all the feelings I wanted to dispel and to highlight the ones I did want, I drew a sun with rays shooting out of it. At the end of each ray I wrote the feelings I wanted to have.

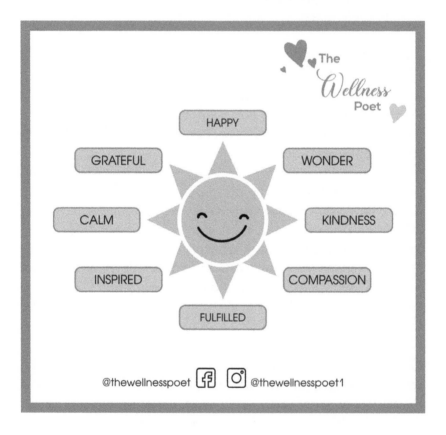

Writing down the feelings I wanted in this way gave me focus and the intention to achieve them. It meant acknowledging when they came up and being aware of myself, especially when I was interacting with others.

I could carry on reading my journal to you, or just photocopy my journal and stick the pages in here. The point I'm trying to make is that with journaling there are no rules, but there are real benefits. When it comes to clearing up your mental and emotional baggage and making sense of your own internal state, which is ultimately reflected in your external state, a journal can shine a light on your soul and help propel you in the right direction to change.

"I realised my body was broken and sore because my insides were broken and sore."

Writing in a journal helps you see yourself more clearly. It's only through our own self-awareness, including the good, bad and ugly, that you can start to have a better relationship with yourself and others. Often your ego does not show up in your journal – he's the guy or girl that tells you you're brilliant and that everyone else is crazy, messed up, wrong, unhappy and you are just perfect as you are. Egos don't really belong in journals – they are usually linked to people's vision board of material things, and I have quite strong feelings about vision boards for material things. I prefer a vision board for health, happiness and love for others.

Now go ahead and tell your ego to f-off and write down your real thoughts and emotions. I call it an emotional deep dive. This deep dive will show you some insights you can be proud of, some you can work on and hopefully clear a path for you to live a better life with yourself and others.

This is Step 1 in going from *Broken to Unbreakable* – you've spent 30 days looking at yourself in a mirror and you've bared your heart and soul, perhaps relived some trauma and past hurts and realised that you might need some help and support to get back to a place that is happier, kinder and freer of all the baggage you've carried with you your entire life. It doesn't matter how broken you are or are not, writing it down will help you fix it.

The very first poem I wrote in my journal was called *Me* and it was all the questions I had about myself after just a few short weeks of journaling. This poem helped me see clearly what I wanted to focus my energy working on for the coming months ahead, and I go back to it whenever I need a reminder of where I've come from.

Now please go buy yourself a beautiful journal or a simple note pad that you will want to carry around in your handbag/backpack and write down anything you think of when the time arises. In committing to this step, you will open an endless vault of opportunities and wonder and begin to view yourself with more curiosity and courage. Only when we are truly open and vulnerable with ourselves do we grow and create space for change.

In Step 1, write in your journal for 30 days.

You can copy my insights from your own perspective to get you started or just start doodling. A thought, emotion or feeling will appear on the page in front of you, and once the flood gates are open you will love learning about yourself and understanding what makes you tick! You can then start to project manage yourself to find the best version of you.

After the 30 days, continue to journal on a regular basis throughout the upcoming steps. This new habit is both insightful and good practice.

Now you are ready for Step 2!

Step 1 Recap

1. Write in your journal for 30 days.

2. Write down your values.

3. Write down the feelings you have the most or common themes.

4. Write down the feelings you wish to have or aspire to feel.

5. Conduct your own emotional deep dive.

"Journaling is a window into your soul that showcases what is in your mind, what is wrong with your body and where to find your spirit."
- The Wellness Poet

"A personal journal is an ideal environment in which to 'become'. It is a perfect place for you to think, feel, discover, expand, remember, and dream."
- Brad Wilcox

Me

Why is my body so sore?
Why don't I laugh anymore?
Oh where, oh where has all my zen gone?
When did it all go wrong?

I'm looking for calm,
With panic and alarm,
It's all in the hips,
Where my negativity sits.

I want love, joy and grace,
A smiling, happy face,
To be brave, calm and strong,
Not ruminate the wrong.

I'm practising self-compassion,
It's really in fashion,
I want joy in my heart,
And to not give a fart.

I have enough,
I am enough,
I am kind,
I am free,
I AM me!

@thewellnesspoet   @thewellnesspoet1

STEP 2

Filing

Marie Kondo says that decluttering will change your life and, to a large extent, I agree. After 15 years of living abroad I decided after the birth of my second child that it was time to pack up our lives and head home. Since I'd lived more than half my adult life abroad and had two babies in a foreign country, there was a lot to organise and plan – a real challenge for the project manager and insomniac within.

I made a plan and sat at a computer for three weeks with the baby asleep in the carrier and I applied for visas, passports, police clearance reports, medical records and so on. I used this time to also organise 15 years of filing in order to have all the relevant papers to hand and upload to the Australian Immigration Portal.

After the paperwork was completed I moved on to packing up the family home in the UK, the shipping container and booking transit for all our belongings. Followed by the research to find a house in Australia, a school and to register for Medicare, Customer Reference Numbers and all the other essential stuff. It was a painful nightmare, at times incredibly stressful, but also cathartic to declutter a whole period of your life in one fell swoop.

On the day the shipping container was loaded, I stood and watched as every last inch of space was filled and the container closed with a bang! My entire adult life fitted into one 20ft container, but the most precious baggage were the two little girls in my hand luggage.

A few months after this experience was over and the shipping container had been unpacked in a rental house Down Under, I had my physical and emotional breakdown. It came at a time that was least expected and was triggered by an event that I probably would have coped well with in normal circumstances. It rocked me, and after years and months of holding it all together, through good times and bad, it all came pouring out. At traffic lights, when I was alone in the car, I would descend into floods of tears.

Farewell to England after 15 years!

@thewellnesspoet 🅕 📷 @thewellnesspoet1

I sought help and my GP suggested antidepressants and gave me the names of three I may benefit from. After an hour researching these antidepressants, I decided that it was not the path for me. I had been sleep-deprived for almost five long years and the idea of feeling manic and suicidal as a side effect to drugs was the most abhorrent consideration I could imagine. What I really needed was a month of continuous sleep and a team of massage therapists on call. My body ached all over and I was so tired it sometimes felt as if I just might die.

When I decided Step 2 was dedicated to filing, it was in part to review all that I had in my life – materially, relationally, emotionally and spiritually – but also to declutter years of built up emotions and frustrations, such as those I shared in Step 1.

The emotional declutter started, and the filing and sorting and making sense of all the stuff I had kept in my emotional basement suddenly seeped out and then erupted like a volcano into my daily life.

I turned to the journal and wrote down all my emotions from the most recent to those long ago, and then I was able to sort them into piles according to different areas of my life. There were some crossovers, some standalone ones and some realisations of long-ago unprocessed traumas. Plus acknowledging I had PTSD from the birth of my children. I had already decluttered the possessions in my life a few months earlier, so it made sense that in Step 2 I sort out the emotional baggage in my life. I decided that until I had dealt with that, there was no way to move forward or lay any kind of new foundations. I wanted the foundations of my life to be strong emotionally, physically and mentally.

A few years ago, I remember thinking it was pointless to start new year's resolutions on the 1st of January, as the month is long and resolutions usually fail by day 10. The best thing to do in January each year is to reflect on the year that has gone and review what you learned, achieved and would like to carry forward to the next year. Therefore, I tend to wait until February to start any new resolutions.

In January I had written down the steps to laying a new foundation to coincide with each month, so I had a clear plan of what was going to happen for the remainder of the year. In Step 1, I reflected on thoughts, feelings, emotions and life. In Step 2, I sorted through my wanted and unwanted feelings and determined what was useful and what wasn't: this was a fundamental step.

Taking accountability for our feelings and emotions is something that we don't often do, as we tend to blame others for how we are feeling. I've learnt that this is wasted energy as we are fully in control of how we think and feel. As a good friend told me, "We can think about our emotions and we can get emotional about our thinking!" and this is so true. We think so much, we often let our emotions spiral out of control. I have been guilty of this for a long time as an over-thinker. Filing my thoughts and feelings allowed me to recognise what I was giving my energy to and what I would prefer to give my energies to.

It's very hard to be subjective about ourselves as we all have an internal critic who judges and tells us we are not as good as we think we are or should be. My internal critic did not allow me to view myself with loving eyes – I was a master at deflecting gratitude. When someone complimented me or gave me a heartfelt thanks, I was very mistrustful of their motives.

Deflecting gratitude is a very common thing and we probably aren't even aware we do it on a daily basis. Coupled with looking for things to go wrong instead of noticing all the things that are right, this is the basis of a lot of anxiety and stress.

To file your emotions and feelings, start by writing them down. It will surprise you that once you write a few and mull on them for a few days, the flood gates will open. Don't worry if you can't come up with an extensive list, chances are they will come to you bit by bit. Keep reviewing what you have written and, as patterns start to emerge, then reflect on your life and which ones relate to certain events and what you learned or experienced during that time.

Reflection is a valuable tool, rumination is not! Rumination is a waste of energy. I've spent years ruminating crappy situations that happened in my life without taking accountability for them or actually trying to understand what I learnt and could have done differently next time. I've always reflected on my work learnings, and I've used reflection and visualisation to learn skills for sporting pursuits, but I've really never done that in respect of relationships or emotions.

For the last decade, I realised I had lived somewhat in a self-help void, floating adrift from the likes of Eckhart and Oprah and all the enlightened, conscious people on earth. I didn't have time, energy or passion for such pursuits. It wasn't a priority, it wasn't in my frame of reference. I had no desire to engage in hippy dippy or woo woo stuff.

This is quite normal for many people who are existing, surviving and working their way through life, bouncing from one stressful job to another. They may have never heard of self-care or the word wellness, and believe it is a luxury for lazy people.

Yes, it's true, I actually believed that only lazy people who were afraid of hard work had time to go to the gym and spruik about wellbeing. Now I know what an idiot I was! A little bit like those people who love filing and everything is always super organised and neat... those people aren't engaged in the real world. OK, so maybe I'm being a little tongue in cheek! I was very good at organising everyone else's projects – I was just in denial and neglect of my own.

So why do we spend Step 2 filing? After Step 1, which was a look into your soul, you need to decide what to do with that stuff:

- Share it to help others.
- Shred it and let go.
- Store it and learn from the experience.

We often take a very common sense approach to practical areas of our life, like buying a house or applying for a new job. I'm not sure we apply the same common sense approach to our feelings and emotions, and perhaps if we did view them as something to be decluttered and sorted out every now and then, they wouldn't smack us in the face several years or even decades down the line.

I mentioned traumas earlier and this process was very helpful for me to recognise the big impact that fertility treatment had on my emotional state over a long period of time. The anxiety, the pain, the suffering and the grief of losing a baby was still in my body. I was so busy existing, working, caring for a baby and young child, I was in no state to make sense of all that had happened. After I organised my emotional thinking and feelings, I was able to pinpoint exactly what it was that was causing my ongoing suffering in my life and what lessons I could learn from those things that had helped me.

Filing does not mean locking something in a cabinet for five to 10 years and hoping that you won't get audited. It's actually taking each emotion and looking at it to assess it for its value and purpose in your life, and then you can decide if you really need it or it's taking up space for more important things you wish to experience. You become accountable for your emotions.

The interesting thing about this is, once you free up space by filing and decluttering your feelings and emotions, you have the opportunity to experience so much more of the things you love and the feelings that give you pleasure. It's not to say that the pain isn't valuable and serves its own purpose, but until you really understand the cause and effect of those pains, you will be stuck re-living the same sad painful stories over and over again and not allow anything new and fresh to enter your life.

I understand clearly now that ruminating on old grievances and allowing my traumas to keep me in a state of anxiety and suffering was blocking me. Not only was I emotionally and mentally stuck, but I was also physically stuck.

To file your own feelings or emotions, think about the following:

- What traumas or losses have you had in your life and what was the impact of them?
- What determines your sense of self-worth and how did this come about?
- What do you ruminate about?
- What have your hardships taught you?
- What kind of person do you think you are?
- What kind of person would others say you were?
- What are the feelings you've experienced over the past few years and what were they related to?
- What makes you angry, sad, frustrated, hurt, happy, joyful, scared and so on?

Write the answers in your journal and then take time to analyse them. Maybe you need to do some research into why people ruminate, or why you feel angry, who has hurt you and what that suffering has taught you.

Taking 30 days (or 28/29 if you stick to a calendar month) to file your life in this way is very cleansing as well as cathartic, because you are taking ownership and accountability for your emotional health and gaining insights into areas where you may be stuck.

Obviously, you may not need to physically be writing things down for 30 days, but you will be reflecting, reconciling and making decisions about what has been beneficial and useful to you. Once you've started to put them to paper and have read over them a few times you will start to become more comfortable with yourself.

This is a scary place for some people to go, I get that. Think of it as all the unpaid bills you've just ignored for years and at some stage they are going to come back and bite your butt. Finding a non-judgemental sounding board for your personal baggage and your untold story could help make sense of things. Statistics could also help you see that you are not alone in your pain!

If you've been lucky and lived a relatively pain-free life then this step may not be as big for you. The truth is you can't skip it because until you understand your thinking and feeling, you really can't move forward with your doing. There will always be something, even for the most privileged of us, because we humans are masters at finding things which cause us to suffer.

Sadly, children are not explained the role of suffering and that others around them may be suffering equally. They don't understand that it's what we do with that suffering that will have the greatest impact on us long term. In school, we generally don't get taught about the role of human emotions and how to make sense of them, or what empathy is in the face of another's personal tragedy. This is a huge shame, and while kindness has become a buzz word at many schools today, I would like to see more education to help young people understand the normal range of human emotion and what it feels like when we suffer stress, loss or trauma.

According to Buddhism, there are two types of growth. Growth through pain and growth through insight! Sometimes we need the pain in order to have the insight. For me, they are linked. Insights come through research and analysing information – if we've not experienced pain then how can we understand it, learn from it and grow as people? Filing enables these insights and can allow us to better understand ourselves and others, which leads to both personal growth and self-acceptance.

In a broad sense, this concept of filing allows self-acceptance as you see yourself as you truly are, good or bad or unsure, and you can determine your direction and areas you want to work on, such as forgiveness, love, compassion, judgement and so on.

A wise woman, Pema Chodron, coined a phrase, "Just Like Me!". If you are vulnerable enough to admit your suffering or acknowledge your struggles you will find someone nearby "Just Like Me".

Sadly, the statistics for most traumas are incredibly high, along with the knowledge that stress is the root cause of most disease. If you've suffered trauma, are still living with trauma and supress your trauma without acceptance and forgiveness, then your body will store that trauma as energy and it will stay inside of you causing you to become very ill over time. The range of traumas is so varied, but the effects can be the same.

Here are some shocking statistics about traumas as well as depression. Sometimes the two are closely linked.

Statistics for miscarriage:

A pregnancy loss is the loss of a fetus that occurs before 20 weeks of gestation. A stillbirth is pregnancy loss that happens any time after 20 weeks.

- If a woman knows about the pregnancy, the risk of loss is about 10% to 15%.
- After week six, the rate of loss is just 5%. It is possible to detect a heartbeat on an ultrasound around week six.
- In the second half of the first trimester, the rate of miscarriage is between 2% and 4%.

Statistics for sexual abuse:

According to CASA (Centres Against Sexual Assault), a university study found 20.6% of women and 10.5% of men reported non-penetrative childhood sexual abuse by the age of 16 and that 7.9% of women and 7.5% of men reported penetrative childhood sexual abuse by the age 16 years.

- 15% of women have been sexually assaulted by a known person compared to 4% who were assaulted by a stranger (Australian Bureau of Statistics – Personal Safety Survey, 2012).

Statistics for women suffering depression:

According to Beyond Blue, one in six women in Australia will experience depression and one in three women will experience anxiety during their lifetime.

- Women also experience post-traumatic stress disorder (PTSD) and eating disorders at higher rates than men.

Statistics for suicide:

According to Suicide Call Back Service, a 24-hour phone and online counselling service, suicides in Australia are the 13th leading cause of death nationally.

- Suicide is the leading cause of death for people aged 15 to 44.
- Male suicide rates in Australia are three times higher than those for women.

These shocking and confronting truths can't be played down, judged or left unheard. For anyone that has experienced trauma or depression, remember to seek help and share your story with others. Shame dies when stories are told in safe spaces.

The final realisation for me during 30 days of Step 2 was that I did not prioritise the following things: family admin, my own wellbeing, my medical appointments or healthy eating. This went a long way to explaining why my physical health was in such a poor state of affairs, including breast cysts, adrenal fatigue, sciatica, muscular aches and pains, low energy, bloating, gas, congested skin, hair loss and mood swings.

"Wow, sounds pretty!" I did not feel pretty and I certainly did not feel healthy! You might think classic new mum, hormonal, post baby blues, but in hindsight I do not believe this. I believe it was endemic of my years of self-neglect, PTSD, ignored messy feelings and emotions. I had so few self-care priorities that I was on the fast track to some kind of chronic disease.

To help clarify, it is now recognised that women can experience PTSD as a result of trauma around the birth of their children. PTSD is not just exclusively for ex-service men and women. Not only did I experience the grief of losing one of my twins at nine weeks, I then had an immensely complicated and difficult pregnancy and delivery. I had clearly seen and heard her heartbeat at six weeks and imagined my life as a mum of twins for a further six weeks before the 12-week scan showed one healthy waving baby and one twisted pretzel that had not grown. This was devastating and the grief was immense.

After crying for two days, I put my game face on and went back to work, pretending everything was fine. Most people did not know I was pregnant. I know I'm not alone and there are thousands of women "Just Like Me!". At the time I did not have a support network that understood what I was going through during the IVF, during the miscarriage and during the subsequent ICP (Intrahepatic Cholestasis of Pregnancy) illness and long, frightening delivery.

I share this dark side in the hope that if you feel even just a little bit broken inside or out, that you take some time to audit yourself inside and out! Pushing ourselves to breaking point is so common and, too often, it's too late for people before they make any changes significant enough to prevent chronic disease or early death and this is very upsetting to me.

Considerations for filing:

- An emotional declutter is as important as a physical declutter!

- Sorting through your emotional baggage will help you understand how much stuff you have.

- Grouping feelings and emotions that are linked by certain events will help you understand what keeps coming up for you and why.

- Understand what sustains you and what drains you. For a helpful explanation you can watch a demonstration on my YouTube channel, *Krissy Regan, The Wellness Poet.* https://bit.ly/SustainersAndDrainers

- Talking through your emotions with a non-judgemental person or therapist will help you understand what feelings are rational and what feelings may be irrational.

- Make time to file and reflect on your emotions and feelings on a regular basis. This will give you a better understanding of what is coming up for you and why you may be reacting in a certain way.

- Start decluttering your room, your cupboards and your house. Shed some of the weight of your possessions, but do not just put them in landfill – recycle, upcycle, donate, share. Start with one room at time and over the next 10 steps you will have let go of a heck of a lot of physical baggage, as well as emotional baggage. And if in doubt about where to start, pick up a copy of Marie Kondo's *The Life-Changing Magic of Tidying Up* and be inspired.

Step 2 Recap

1. Make a list of what sustains you and what drains you and develop a personalised self-care plan.

2. Start the process of decluttering your emotions and your living space.

3. Review statistics relevant to your life and consider the impacts of that on your thoughts and behaviour.

4. Decide what you want to do with all your STUFF:

   • Share it to help others.

   • Shred it and let go.

   • Store it and learn from the experience.

5. Remember there are many people "Just Like Me!".

"Enjoy the peace of nature and declutter your inner world."

- Amit Ray

"To forgive is to set a prisoner free and discover that the prisoner was you."

- Lewis B. Smedes

Filing your Life

To file is not to pile a mountain of stuff so vast,
To declutter is not to flutter on what you found in the past,
To shred is not to dread all the stories of long ago,
To clean is not to mean that your memories must go,
To sort, to sweep, to dust, to tidy, to arrange, to adjust,
All this stuff can hold you back and it's not so easy to pack,
Our fears and our hopes with our trophies and our soaps,
We must make room, so take a bag and a broom,
There are opportunities trapped under your bed,
In your life, your heart and in your head,
You can find a fresh new life, free from dust, debris and strife.

STEP 3

Mindfulness

Trends come and go but as far as mindfulness goes, I think it's here to stay and will only continue to grow. Mindfulness is now taught in prisons, schools and mental health sectors, and it allows people to recognise and label their thoughts without attaching judgement to them. The main idea is that we are not our thoughts and our thoughts are only a part of us. When we create space between us and our thoughts, we don't become consumed by them, mentally being dragged into whatever is going on in our head based on our worries, feelings or emotions. Now, of course, our mind is useful for problem-solving, planning, creating and remembering, but the reality is we actually use so little of our thinking time to do this.

It is documented that humans have over 70,000 thoughts per day, and 98% of them we have had before. When I read this staggering statistic, my first thoughts were 'how bloody boring'. We think about the same crap over and over. When do we have time to think of new stuff? Only 2% of the time?

I am a classic over-thinker of the 98%, and it strikes me now how I had very little room in my head to think creatively or grow or learn new stuff. I was stuck in a loop – a constant cycle of the same thoughts, same movies in my head, same conversations, same sufferings. What the heck could I do about it?

Taking an introductory mindfulness course sparked my curiosity and gave me the basic tools I needed to understand mindfulness. My thirst for knowledge ensured I knew what to do with the information and where to seek out more content that could help me better understand myself and others. Following Step 1 and Step 2, hopefully you have now identified some of the things you think or feel on a regular basis. Once you have that information, the key is understanding what you want to do about it.

In Step 3, we will discuss this and look at some practical examples that you can employ to manage your thoughts and emotions and understand your thinking patterns.

As mentioned already, I had spent much of the past 10 years living in a state of constant stress. Since the birth of my children I was in flight or fight mode every minute of every day. For other people, such as my employers and colleagues, I was generally able to function to a high standard, but at home I found basic stuff like doing the laundry or the constant pile of dishes in the kitchen caused me a lot of anxiety. It all felt very overwhelming at times, being needed on so many levels. These feelings continued for some years and I had no understanding of mindfulness or its practical application to everyday worries.

We spend a lot time of engaging in our thoughts and invest energy in recreating the same stories over and over. Most of us experience life largely spent in a mode of "doing" as opposed to "being" and it's when we spend too much time doing that life becomes overwhelming and stressful.

When we are in doing mode, we are generally planning, worrying, ruminating and being active. The opposite, which is 'being' mode, is more receptive, accepting and we allow things to be without over analysing. By focusing on the present moment and having more body and breath awareness, we allow ourselves just to BE!

It takes time to understand and practise this skill and to notice your own responses to various situations. Once you have understood the difference between doing and being, you do find yourself wanting to spend more time in being and less time doing and the real skill is to move seamlessly between the two.

The great thing about being mode is that you have fewer thoughts because you are present in the here and now. Stressful thoughts can creep in, and when they do, you can look at them more objectively.

Let's consider an example:

"You are stuck in traffic and likely to be late for work, you start worrying about being late and messing up your day, having to cancel a meeting or letting people down. On top of this, you are tired, haven't slept well and haven't had time to eat. Your mind starts racing with worries and imagined conversations you might have to have because you know now you will be late for work. You also start to feel annoyed that everyone is holding you up, and no-one cares that you are hungry. All of a sudden, the whole world is against you and your heart is racing and you start pumping adrenaline around your body as your body thinks you may be in danger and it needs to get ready to fight or flight. The traffic lights change to red and you start banging on your horn, annoyed with the dude in front who should have sped through the lights.

You are now starting to get ropable. You start imagining getting out of your car and abusing the dude in front for being an idiot – and on and on! You can see where this story may go. But actually, what happens is that you get every green light the rest of the way to work, you arrive on time and have a few minutes to grab a coffee before going to your desk. You pull yourself together and pretend to be human and in control – the crisis was averted."

Did you feel your heart rate go up reading this story? Mine did! So, here's how we can play this story out differently using some mindfulness techniques:

"You are stuck in traffic and likely to be late for work, you start worrying about being late and messing up your day, having to cancel a meeting or letting people down. On top of this you are tired, haven't slept well and haven't had time to eat. You notice that you are starting to feel edgy about being late for work and you feel a bit annoyed you haven't had time for breakfast. You acknowledge these thoughts by saying to yourself, 'I feel tired, edgy and I'm worried about being late! Perhaps I could have been more organised this

morning. Don't worry, I'm safe and I will get to work on time, there is no point stressing about it now!' You look out of the window at the traffic lights, notice the trees are in bloom, or your favourite song is on the radio and take four deep breaths.

The driver in front of you is a bit slow taking off when the lights change and you smile and think he must be having a rough morning too. You get every green light and make it to the office on time. As you buy your coffee, you comment to the person at the counter that the trees along the side of the road have such amazing flower blooms and it was really beautiful to see them on the drive to work, you wish them a nice day and go to your desk. No imagined crisis, no worries, no increased heart rate. In fact, you have connected with nature and another human being and averted a physiological response (adrenaline spike and increased heart rate) to an imagined event. Your body and your mind did not become stressed, because you just stayed present in the moment and did not let your mind run wild."

Do you feel calm and full of compassion and love for nature and the person in the car in front of you, as well as the person who made your coffee? I do!

The above example is a practical look at something we are faced with every day. To understand mindfulness, it's good to understand how our brain works and how we respond to stress.

Our brains are wired to make decisions, which recognise threats and keep us safe. This goes back to our caveman days when we were all being chased, and perhaps eaten, by wild animals or other tribes. Nowadays, the threats are a boss who micromanages us or provides no leadership whatsoever, a jealous co-worker, screaming kids, Christmas shopping, school fees, paying your rent/mortgage, juggling family's expectations with your own and navigating relationships on a multitude of levels.

Whilst these may not be life threatening on a day-to-day basis, your body and your mind does not know that and so it reacts physiologically and emotionally as if you may be "eaten" at any moment when encountering stressful situations.

We will talk more about perceived stress versus real stress later, but for now let's consider some practical examples of what we have covered so far.

When our bodies are in a constant state of stress, they produce hormones such as adrenaline, cortisol and norepinephrine to help with our flight or fight response. Too much of these hormones activated regularly in our body over a long period of time, can cause our adrenal glands to become burnt out. This can lead to adrenal fatigue or adrenal burnout, which manifests in the body in many different ways. Too much cortisol can suppress the immune system, increase blood pressure and sugar, decrease libido, produce acne, contribute to obesity and more.

The physiological response we have to perceived threats versus actual threats is the same, your body does not know the difference between a thought of an attack or an actual attack, it responds in the same way. Our body will release energy and hormones to prepare to fight or run. This came as quite a shock to me, because I spent a large proportion of my personal and professional life anticipating the worst-case scenario and then planning and finding ways to prevent it from happening and keeping people safe. I never switched it off. This meant that all my energy was focused on the outer world, perceived threats versus real threats, and as a result my body was suffering.

As I mentioned earlier, during my pregnancy with my eldest child, I developed a rare and serious condition called Intrahepatic Cholestasis of Pregnancy (ICP) which was life threatening for the baby and immensely uncomfortable to me in many ways, including chronic sleep deprivation, a burning itch all over my body and my blood chemistry and liver function went wild. I was desperately worried about losing her, as she was a twin pregnancy and I had already lost the other baby at nine weeks. I lay in bed every night thinking and googling, worrying, itching and sometimes crying. I just about survived this condition for 10 weeks and when I could manage no more, I begged the consultant to end my suffering and my baby was delivered at 36 weeks and taken to special care. These first seven days were far from straightforward for either of us but, thank God, she was alive.

After I took her home from hospital the choking started, as did my PTSD. She choked all the time, day and night for no reason! For the first three years of her life I did not sleep much. I would wake whenever I heard her breathe funny. I created the classic rod for my already broken back, which was to spend many hours night and day nursing her and being as close as possible to her. I also understood firsthand why sleep deprivation is used as a form of torture, you lose your mind and your ability to function and you want it to end. I arrived home with a newborn baby with 10 sleepless weeks already under my belt.

There were many scary choking moments in those first three years and I did not have any mindfulness skills to draw on to calm me down and bring my body back to homeostasis (in balance). It's very hard to live in a constant state of fear, but I'm not ashamed to say that I'm sure my hyper-vigilant state and running the stairs three at a time may have saved her life on many occasions.

During my mindfulness course I had a huge aha moment when I realised that the fear that I had lived in for all those years had actually kept her safe. It was because I had a fear of losing her that I worried and did all the things I did. As a result, she was safe, she survived the most fragile years of her life and is now a very active and bouncing child.

I was able to thank fear for helping me take care of her and to acknowledge the role it had played in my life over the five years. I then told that fear to "take a holiday". I don't need you right now, I'm done being scared and burned out. I'm not denying it was bloody hard work and had taken a huge toll on my body and my mind.

If you have lived in fear, experienced loss or trauma, your body probably responded the same way mine did, which was to stay on high alert for further danger and trauma. This is dangerous for your long-term health and your current health. You can talk to a professional to get some counselling, you can attend a mindfulness course near you, or you can take some time to write down your feelings, your fears and your worries and put them into some kind of perspective as we talked about in Step 1 and 2. Often being aware of the impact of our thoughts, feelings and stressors is enough to help people change the way they feel about certain things.

I mentioned already that stress is the leading cause of illness and disease according to the World Health Organization. In this step, we looked at some examples of stressful moments in life, such as traffic, personal conflict and grief.

In Step 3, I want you to start to practise noticing and being aware of your daily thoughts. What are you thinking about most of the time? What is causing your angst, frustration and what movie is playing in your head?

Write it down and ask yourself:

1. Is it real?
2. Is it perceived?
3. Is it helpful?
4. Is it part of my 98%?

Then as you start to notice more and more of your 98%, you can change your internal narrative, shut it off or thank it for helping you and move on. As you become more accustomed to doing this over the 30 days, when you notice a 98 percenter you can bring your attention to the present moment by focusing on breathing, looking at some trees or the smile on your child's face and you instantly get out of your head. It gets you out of the 98% and you start to create more space and distance between the things that are not helpful, interesting or real.

Eckhart Tolle's book *The Power of Now* teaches us a lot about living in the present. I've found it an immensely valuable resource, drawing on his experience and its application to daily life. Having children tests you in every way, and often you just might not feel like you are going to get through the day after a very long and sleepless night.

Since learning mindfulness, when I'm faced with a situation that is challenging and frustrating, I make a deal with myself: if I can stay present during this next hour and get through this difficult moment with compassion and grace, I will reward myself with something just for me. I make pacts with myself.

An example of this, was when my 20-month-old (at the time) was going through a phase of getting car sick regularly and projectile vomiting in her seat while I was driving. This is stressful, as you have to find a place to stop safely, jump out and run around and remove her from the car seat while trying to prevent her from choking on her vomit and getting covered in the foul-smelling stuff. During the initial period of trying to stop the car, get her out and contain the damage, I'm in flight/saviour/fixer mode, then the crying usually starts (her, not me) as she realises she has been sick all over herself and she feels awful. I feel like crying too, but I try to hold it together on the side of the road.

After a few episodes of this you do become more prepared with towels, cleaning product and spare clothes in the car within reach, so you can manage on the side of the road if you have to. On this particular day, it happened on the way home from day care just around the corner from my house. After initially dealing with the safety of it, I drove us home and got the kids out of the car and once again went to get a bucket and cleaning materials, while wondering how the hell a car that was only 12 months old would survive its seven-year warranty at this rate.

Rather than get annoyed or feel sorry for myself that yet again my afternoon could have been better spent, I told myself, "This too shall pass, just breathe and try not to think too much about what happened because I can't change it, so there is no point worrying or being upset". I took several long and slow deliberate breaths while sponging the vomit off the fabric (not a great idea in hindsight as the smell was appalling). I felt much better about just dealing with this moment and what was in front of me and not allowing all the other jobs, still waiting to be done, to cause me stress and anxiety.

Mindfulness has been proven to:

- Reduce stress.
- Increase health and wellbeing.
- Increase our capacity and coping mechanisms.
- Create awareness of our mind and thinking.
- Enable acceptance and non-resistance to things we can't control.
- Improve relationships with self and others.
- Improve relaxation and sleep.

I certainly feel that this is all true for me and, as a sufferer of insomnia for most of my life, my new ability to not ruminate, detach from my thinking and be calmer and more relaxed has immensely improved what little sleep I was getting. I also decided to prioritise sleep above all things, so I gave up watching TV and created a bedtime routine that started as soon as the kids went to bed. This helped me wind down and fall asleep much more easily.

My bedtime routine is as follows:

- Kids in bed.
- House lights go down and lock up the house.
- Shower and put on pjs.

- Stretching for 30–40 minutes whilst listening to meditative, relaxing music.
- Gratitude ritual of thanking my body for all it has done for me today and gratitude for all the things in my life.
- Go to bedroom, devices off and in another room, lights down, read for 20 minutes.
- Sleep.

If my mind starts to think and race, I say to it:

"Thank you for all you have done for me today, but I don't need you right now. My brain needs to rest, so please go to sleep."

Then I focus on deep breathing for as long as it takes to fall asleep. If I need to repeat this statement to myself a few times I do so, but usually I don't have to say it more than once. As a long-term "night thinker" this new-found skill is my most valuable.

I also believe that a huge shift in my health and wellbeing occurred the moment I acknowledged the role fear had played in my life for so long and the impact it had on my body. When I thanked fear and asked it to take a holiday, my body and mind quickly started to repair itself. You could try the same with grief, anger, hurt, frustration, grievances and forgiveness for someone that wronged you.

The principle is the same:

1. Acknowledge the emotion.
2. Notice how it made you feel all this time.
3. Recognise the impact it has had on your life.
4. Understand the effect it has had on you physically and mentally.
5. Thank the emotion for its role in your life and what it has taught you, then ask it to take a holiday!

When we become more mindful, we naturally have increased capacity and coping mechanisms. After a long time of feeling overwhelmed through exhaustion and lack of control, it's wonderful to try and regain some of that lost coping ability.

Our minds are very powerful, but also very harmful when left unchecked. There is a lot of research currently to show that we have the power to influence our physiology and our genes by what we think about.

Dr Joe Dispenza is a leading authority on this topic, and in my opinion, he is doing amazing things with everyday people, as well as disillusioned medical professionals who have been taught to write prescriptions and have not had the training to deal with health in a more holistic way. Of course, there are lots of amazing medical professionals helping sick people. But what if we flipped it and we weren't helping sick people, but we actually helped people stay well and prevented them from becoming sick in the first place through their thoughts, actions, habits and choices.

Everybody's idea of health and wellness is different and we are all drawn to certain kinds of foods and fads and have our favourite things. I was shocked when I asked a staff member in the supermarket about a wholefoods product and her response was, she didn't know, she likes "real food" too much. By this she meant processed food, as opposed to wholefood ingredients that you have to cook, with actual nutritional value.

I've decided NOT to sit on the fence with my new-found feelings and understanding of food. As I became more mindful of my thinking and my health, I became very mindful about what I put into my body. Most food manufacturers and supermarkets put profits before our health.

I have chosen my health over the profits of companies that do not care if they poison their shoppers, causing cancer and type 2 diabetes en masse.

This is another effect of mindfulness; you start to actually give a crap about yourself and what you put into your body. Fairly soon you will start to educate yourself more about food, nutrition and health, and make choices that will benefit you in the long term. Of course, you will still enjoy treats sometimes, but you will also enjoy a whole range of new healthy foods, with increased energy, increased health, weight loss and you will be able to think more clearly and sleep better. It's up to you, the choice is yours. I think by the end of this book you will be making good choices!

If you feel uninformed about food and the impact it has on your health there are a lot of brilliant documentaries on Netflix, YouTube and Food Matters TV. Just be curious and start watching and you will become more mindful of creating a better lifestyle for yourself.

You will find a copy of my *Top 20 Health and Wellness Tips* at the back of this book on page 171.

Step 3 Recap

1. Note down what you think about 98% of the time.

2. Think about what drives your emotional reactions.

3. Acknowledge the role certain emotions have played in your life and, if appropriate, ask them to take a holiday.

4. Practise mindfulness relative to your life.

5. Set a bedtime routine for yourself.

"The first step in crafting the life you want is to get rid of everything you don't."
- Joshua Becker

"Nothing in life is to be feared, it is only to be understood. Now is the time to understand more, so that we may fear less."
- Marie Curie

"He who has overcome his fears will truly be free."
- Aristotle

"There is only one thing that makes a dream impossible to achieve: the fear of failure."
- Paulo Coelho

Anticipation

Anticipation is an occupation that does not pay the rent,
To anticipate is to speculate on what you might be sent,
It's fun to hope and wonder but try not to lament,
A positive mind will help minimise all that energy spent.

When you catch yourself caught up in the past,
Do not ruminate on what you did last,
Take a moment to find your breath,
Let go the emotion that catches in your chest.

Your life is right here in the present,
You don't have to worry what might be sent,
There's calm to be found, so shift the doubts that bound,
Create space in your head, find stillness and presence
instead.

@thewellnesspoet @thewellnesspoet1

STEP 4

Appreciation

To feel truly appreciated in life is one of the most wonderful feelings, when we allow ourselves permission to accept it. Too often we deflect gratitude and when people thank us, it can feel a bit empty. Appreciation, thanks or gratitude are part of a new way of living for people who have decided to incorporate "gratitude practice" into their daily life. This may be just a cooler way of saying grace, or saying our thank you prayers at night, and for those less-religious people it can be done with no specific religious agenda.

The rituals of saying grace before a meal or saying some thank you prayers before we go to bed have largely been lost in our modern, hectic world, but the realities and benefits are exactly the same. I'm not saying it's a fad, as actually I believe wholeheartedly that when we are grateful, we allow space for good things to come into our life. When you forget to be grateful for the basic air you breathe, food you eat and abundance of opportunities in your life, you are living in a place of scarcity. This means you can't attract positivity, love and abundance in your life.

In Step 4 we are going to consider the importance of appreciation and gratitude in how we live our life, and we will practise it for 30 days.

Once you embed this new habit, you will notice things to be grateful for every time you take a moment to look up. You will carry this new-found appreciation for life into your future.

I want to start first with the idea that many of us deflect gratitude because it brings us some form of discomfort, or we feel there is an agenda behind the person delivering the thanks. What does deflecting gratitude even mean, and why is it important?

Even the nicest, most deserved thank you can catch us off guard, leaving us scrambling to come up with an appropriate response, or we deflect it straight back: "Oh, that was nothing!". We immediately dismiss the appreciation of our efforts and act like it was normal. What you do in that moment is turn the positive energy that has been given to you into negative energy, and the person who delivered the sentiment may think twice about saying it to you again.

You have probably had appreciation scarcity in the past and haven't been taught how valuable your efforts and attention are. Or, you may rush around saying thank you one thousand times a day without stopping to tell those most important to you how much you appreciate them. We do this because we've not been taught, or even practised, the art of gracefully and wholeheartedly accepting appreciation for ourselves and understanding the benefits to ourselves and others.

When we open ourselves up to appreciation, we open ourselves up to receive a whole range of opportunities and benefits. When we show appreciation to others, or practise gratitude for all the good things in our life, we open ourselves up to attract more good things. Positive attracts positive.

Appreciation is defined as: recognition and enjoyment of the good qualities of someone or something.

Gratitude is defined as: the quality of being thankful; readiness to show appreciation for and to return kindness.

According to Psychology Today and an article by Dr Randy Kamen, the *10 Scientifically Proven Benefits for Gratitude* are:

1. Gratitude opens the door to more relationships.
2. Gratitude improves physical health.
3. Gratitude improves psychological health.
4. Gratitude increases empathy and reduces aggression.
5. Grateful people sleep better.
6. Gratitude improves self-esteem.
7. Gratitude increases mental strength and resilience.
8. Gratitude improves self-care and greater likelihood to exercise.
9. Gratitude heightens spirituality – ability to see something bigger than ourselves.

10. Gratitude strengthens your heart, immune system, and decreases blood pressure.

Even in our hardest times, worst times, most tragic and devastating times, being grateful and appreciating what you can will help you recover quickly. It's common to focus on the negative and seeming impossibility of a situation, but if you look hard enough you will find something to be grateful for. This can provide an anchor to keep you steady during the really turbulent times.

I want you to start each morning when you wake up with a daily moment of appreciation. Before you get out of bed, take a few deep breaths and think of something you are grateful for that day.

For some people, that could be as simple as, **"I woke up, I'm still alive!"** and that is extremely important. For others it might be:

"Thank you, my child is no longer ill."
"Thank you, I had a restful sleep."
"Thank you, the neighbour's dog didn't bark all night."
"Thank you for a safe home and comfortable bed and a safe place to sleep."

It can be just one thing, it's quick, it's simple and reminding yourself to do this every morning will make a big impact on how you start your day and open you up to receive fully throughout the day.

The next thing is to find an "appreciation buddy". It could be your partner, your best friend, your sister, brother, etc. Every night before bed, message them the three **things** you are grateful for that day.

Again, they can be simple facts:

"It was not so hot today, I didn't get wet in the rain, I had a great lunch", or, *"I met a friend for coffee, my child was happy at school, my partner did the dishes!"*

The more you notice these small things to be grateful for, the sooner you will find the bigger stuff too.

You can also write your moments of appreciation and gratitude in your journal as mentioned in Step 1. On your harder or more challenging days, if you need inspiration you can go back to your journal and refer to them again.

You will start to feel more positive about life overall and you will moan less about little inconveniences that may have once been a huge drama to you. Moaning about having to drop the kids at school, going to the gym, going to work, making dinner all of a sudden become things to be grateful for, because you GET to do it. You are not dead; you are not lost in the jungle. Daily life becomes an increasing list of things to be grateful for.

Being mindful of our opportunities each day to live and appreciate our choices is such a privilege which gets lost in our hectic, competitive and selfish world.

You may like to start your own little mantra, which will help build your own internal appreciation.

Sit comfortably with your hands on your legs and say to yourself:

"I am grateful for a healthy body!"

Move your hands over your heart and say:

"I am grateful for a happy heart!"

Then put your hands on either side of your head and say:

"I am grateful for a brilliant mind!"

When someone expresses appreciation or thanks to you, DO NOT deflect it. A simple "thank you" will do and you will become more comfortable receiving, as well as giving, appreciation.

If saying thank you feels too short, you can try something like, "Thank you, I appreciate it," or, "Thank you, that means a lot," or, "Thank you, that's so kind!".

If you've not had role models that encouraged you to be grateful and appreciate your life, you will find this quite a big shift. We often tend to focus on the negative in life and dismiss or brush aside the positive.

Nowadays our life is instantaneous. At the tap of a button we enjoy instant gratification for things we buy or want, so it may feel like a backwards step to be grateful for air, water, food and safety. You might even feel you don't have time to practise gratitude and appreciation! If this is the case, you can expect to go through life with challenges, problems, obstacles and a lack of appreciation for yourself.

When was the last time you thanked yourself for showing up, making a difference, caring for someone, doing the shopping, having a job to put food on the table? Thanking yourself is also acknowledging your own efforts, which then makes it easier to notice others.

After you've been practising appreciation for a few weeks you will start to feel calmer, happier, more connected and closer to those around you – even strangers! You will actively look for people to wholeheartedly thank for their efforts in what they do. You will notice other people going out of their way to make life better for others and you will feel immensely grateful to them, and you must find a way to tell them.

Find a way to let people know that you have noticed their efforts, their care and their attention. Our entitled nature and culture have also eroded the value of thanks, because we think it's just par for the course that people do stuff, regardless if they go the extra mile consistently. This can be true in both a work context as well as home, and people quickly feel taken for granted and resentful if they go the extra mile and never get properly (wholeheartedly) thanked and acknowledged for their efforts. Many work and personal relationships quickly deteriorate if this is the case.

There is evidence to say that when we express appreciation and receive the same, our brain releases dopamine and serotonin. These two hormones are crucial neurotransmitters responsible for our emotions, and they make us feel good. They also enhance our mood immediately, making us feel happy on the inside. Do you feel yourself smile when you genuinely thank someone? This is why!

Dr Susan Ferguson says, *"When humans feel gratitude, the brain produces oxytocin, a hormone important to bonding. It stands to reason that not only will we bond more deeply with people when we feel gratitude but we will feel happy and loved"*.

In the same way that appreciation and gratitude positively affect our emotions and hormones, negativity, frustrations and your idea that it's "Me against the world," and, "Nobody loves me!" does too.

Repeated negative thoughts, such as anger, resentment, fear or sadness, causes our bodies to release the stress hormones. Long term, these are damaging to our health, so as well as a mood boost, appreciation is also a health boost.

Now here's an admission of my own, which you can probably relate to as well. As an adult, I was previously rubbish at accepting gratitude from people. It made me immensely uncomfortable. I deflected gratitude and just brushed it off as nothing to write about.

When people tried to show me appreciation verbally, I felt slightly mistrustful that they were doing it to take advantage of my generosity. However, I am also a caretaker, who looks for people to take care of and I give a lot of myself to others. I can become resentful when I feel unappreciated or my efforts are not noticed.

This sounds like two totally conflicting statements. I want to feel appreciated, but when I am, I feel uncomfortable. Perhaps you've noticed this in yourself or others? I have therefore attracted a lot of takers in my life and forgotten how to give to myself first.

Now with all of these realisations, some of which may ring true for you and you may have more of your own, I started to understand where my imbalance for appreciation really was. I was not giving myself the appreciation I deserved. I was making drama out of everyday stuff, rather than being grateful for what I did have. I was resentful of people I'd helped and I'd over-given to takers.

Once I understood this and could set about taking the steps to improve my own relationship with appreciation and gratitude, I started to feel a lot healthier, connected and loved. It did not take long, and you won't want to let those feelings go once you've got them.

If you keep going, keep practising gratitude, keep appreciating what you have, keep thanking your body, mind and heart for helping you and noticing when others are going the extra mile these feelings of love and health will multiply.

And remember to be quick to wholeheartedly thank people in person for going the extra mile, or in writing, whenever and however it feels appropriate. Don't be fake, don't be false, don't expect it in return!

One of the great joys of my life now, that was probably overlooked before, is when my child says thank you to me for everyday things that I do! I never really felt the power of it before, but now my heart sings, my frequency rises, I'm mindful of noticing the expression on their face when they say it and projecting back my appreciation and love to them, to help them understand the value of appreciation.

When my child is stressed, worried, feeling sad, we say some thank you prayers and I know it calms her, helps her feel loved and she sleeps better.

It can be challenging to show appreciation to difficult and toxic people, even when they do things to mean well. Feeling okay about saying thanks to someone who is maybe unkind and unhelpful at times is a test of your strength and resilience. Sometimes you may be faced with timewasters or unhelpful staff on the telephone, or in a shop where you need to resolve an issue. It's hard in these moments to be grateful for those experiences, but you can say to yourself:

"I'm grateful I got to practise compassion and restraint today. I'm grateful that I have choices in my life and even though that person wasted lot of my time, I learnt some things which will be useful for next time."

If you are asked to do a difficult task at work or something you don't like doing, you can reframe it and be grateful for the opportunity to learn a new skill, grateful for the chance to test your thinking and resourcefulness, grateful for the opportunity to show others what you are truly capable of, grateful that you have a job and people value you, which is why you were allocated that task.

This takes practice, but the more mindful you are to look for the angle in which to appreciate each moment, the more content you will be to take on new things and challenge yourself. After 30 days of practising Step 4 you will feel significantly happier and healthier and may even be pre-empting the next steps and taking some actions towards them. Keep your appreciation rituals going, the benefits never go on holiday.

Step 4 Recap

1. Write down what you are grateful for each day and share it with others.

2. Thank people wholeheartedly and openly for their contribution.

3. Start each day with one thing to be grateful for.

4. Role model the importance of appreciation to your family.

5. Create your own little ritual to thank your mind and body for all it does for you and practise regularly.

"Thankfulness is the beginning of gratitude. Gratitude is the completion of thankfulness. Thankfulness may consist merely of words. Gratitude is shown in acts."

- Henri Frederic Amiel

"Gratitude is when memory is stored in the heart and not in the mind."

- Lionel Hampton

"When I started counting my blessings, my whole life turned around."

         - Willie Nelson

"Be thankful for what you have; you'll end up having more. If you concentrate on what you don't have, you will never, ever have enough."

         - Oprah Winfrey

I am Grateful

Thank you for my legs and for all the journeys they have led,
Thank you to for my face and kisses from two angels
Clodagh Rose and Kara Grace,
Thank you for my eyes, ears, nose and mouth, to sense
all the beautiful things in this place,
Thank you for the food in my fridge and water in my bath,
The sea, the river, the moonlight on my path,
Thank you for hope, love and wonder,
Thank you to the people who bring me joy and laughter,
Thank you for each day that comes,
A lesson, a memory, an opportunity to be, aware, happy, kind
and free.

STEP 5

Meditation

Meditation has been practised in different parts of the world for thousands of years. It has become much more popular in the West in recent years, and many high-profile figures, including celebrities, business leaders, sports stars and wellness gurus, talk a lot about the benefits of meditation.

Dr Joe Dispenza is a leading researcher in the field of "Mind over Matter" and healing our bodies from chronic illness through thought alone. This sounds so far out there; most people can't comprehend how to even go about it. But his research has proven that we can use our minds to repair our bodies when channelling the right thoughts. So, what are the right thoughts?

In Step 5 we are going to look at reasons to include meditation as part of your regular routine. We are going to set an intention to meditate every day for 30 days and then going forward you will include this as part of your routine, as much as you can manage.

We are going to consider the benefits, the opportunities and the relationship between mindfulness, meditation and yoga. The fun thing about meditation is that it can be done absolutely anywhere, and it can be as short as one minute or as long as one hour (although some people do meditate for much longer).

For the purpose of this step, I advise meditating for 10-12 minutes each day until you get comfortable with it, and then you can lengthen or shorten as you see fit.

Common reasons people give for not meditating:

1. I'm too busy to meditate.
2. My mind won't keep quiet to meditate.
3. Meditation is too "woo woo" for me.
4. I've tried it once and didn't enjoy it.

According to Healthline.com the *12 Science-Based Benefits of Meditation* are:

1. Reduces stress. Stress reduction is one of the most common reasons people try meditation.
2. Controls anxiety. Less stress translates to less anxiety.
3. Promotes emotional health.
4. Enhances self-awareness.
5. Lengthens attention span.
6. May reduce age-related memory loss.
7. Can generate kindness.
8. May help fight addictions.
9. Improves sleep.
10. Helps control pain.
11. Can decrease blood pressure.
12. You can meditate anywhere.

And here's a few more reasons of my own:

1. Gives your mind a chance to stop with the thinking and clear space for new ideas.
2. Enhances creativity.
3. Allows you to explore your emotions without judgement and negativity.
4. Allows you to transition from one role to the next, e.g. worker to wife to mum to friend.
5. Enables you to gain perspective on matters and aids in making the right decision.
6. Gives your body a chance to tell you what is going on inside when your mind is quiet.
7. It's a chance to listen to your heart and soul about questions in your life.
8. Improves your ability to call on and use your intuition.

To recap from Step 3, let's remind ourselves about mindfulness, which is living in the moment, noticing what is happening and making choices in how you respond to your experience, rather than being driven by habitual reactions.

Mindfulness is the quality of awareness you are seeking to experience quite naturally in everyday life by being present and not catastrophising or thinking negatively about the past or future.

Being mindful means you can create a richer and deeper emotional awareness, which can be described as "heartfulness". Your heart becomes more open to life's ups and downs and you feel more connected to the world around you.

Meditation is the process or time, when you practise cultivating this quality of awareness.

The more you meditate, the more mindful you will become.

Generally, there are considered to be three main types of meditation:

1. **Focused awareness meditation:** watching and quietening the "monkey mind" (the incessant chatter and dialogue in our heads) and using our breath as an anchor to let go of our thoughts. Watching and noticing your breath is very calming. A good trick is to say to your brain, "Monkey, watch breath!". In giving your monkey mind a task to do, you gain some control over it and over time you will need to do this less and less. You can ask your monkey mind to "watch breath", as often as you need to, or when your thoughts start bouncing around in your head again.

2. **Open monitoring meditation:** when your mind is calm and focused, you can observe your experiences with curiosity, like watching your experiences through a GoPro of awareness. This allows you to see everything, including the good and bad, take

it in, see it for what it is and then let it go. You are observing your experiences with curiosity and peace. Usually we try to reject negative experiences, but with this type of meditation you can consider them and decide what is useful and what is not (fact or fiction). This will allow you to participate more fully in your life and not to push aside bad experiences, allowing you to put negative thinking in context. "Oh, I'm experiencing some negative thoughts right now, that's interesting. Do I need to waste my time and energy ruminating or worrying?"

3. **Loving kindness meditation (LKM):** is focused on cultivating a warm and kind attitude to yourself and others. LKM has been shown by science to positively impact your emotions, physical health, sense of connection and even the brain itself. This is a great practice to lead on from Step 4, where we notice and appreciate all that is good in the world and in our life. This meditation helps build your love, tolerance, acceptance, non-judgement and compassion for all beings.

After you've practised meditation for a while you will be able to use all three approaches. Each provides a path towards complete transformation. Then slowly all areas of your life will become infused by mindfulness. At home, at work, with your family, with your friends and with the world around you.

The interesting thing about meditation is that you can ask your soul life's big questions, and usually the answer will come to you! Perhaps not in that exact moment, but fairly soon after.

In my early days of practising meditation, I was doing a guided meditation and the voice was telling me just to accept whatever was coming up for me today. I thought, "Nothing is coming up for me today, I must not be doing it right". Within a few seconds of having this thought, I remembered I had left the oven on at my house around the corner. I jumped up and drove home telling myself to calm down and not visualise the house burning down. Despite not much coming up for me that day, I thanked the meditation for helping me remember this important fact! It still makes me smile when I remember it.

In Step 4 we practised appreciation. Being mindful and meditating regularly enhances your appreciation for life itself.

Transition meditations are very short meditations you can use throughout your day to help you change gears or change roles. In life, we constantly switch roles or change hats, from daughter to friend, sister, mother, colleague, confidant, lover, paramedic, chef, cleaner, taxi driver. Playing so many roles in any given day is very tiring, especially when the switch happens in an instant and you have to jump back and forth throughout the day.

A very useful method to help overcome the mental fatigue of constantly changing roles/hats is to give yourself some times in the day where you do a short transition meditation.

A transition meditation is a quick 60–90 second meditation where you can focus on your breath, acknowledge and appreciate all the things that went well in your day, acknowledge how your body is feeling (thank it for any messages it sends you) and mentally prepare yourself for the next part of your day (or the next role you will assume).

I find the most useful times for this meditation are in those transitional moments when we move from worker to parent to partner (between school drop off and work, arriving home from work after a long day, before picking the kids up and before getting out of bed in the morning).

A typical example for a parent would be to arrive at the school car park five minutes early before pick up, and rather than checking your social media or emails, you can do a quick transition meditation.

> Close your eyes, take 10 deep long breaths and quieten your mind; feeling your body, quietly saying a few things you are grateful for and thanking yourself for getting through your day

so far. Ask your body to let go of any stress and tension. This will take you 2–3 minutes and you will arrive at the classroom door refreshed, less stressed and ready to take on your parenting role.

Another example could be at work before a difficult meeting or an interview, you can prepare yourself by calming your mind and your central nervous system.

Find a quiet place, close your eyes, take 10 deep breaths. Say to yourself, "I trust myself to handle this meeting calmly and professionally. I have all the skills and abilities needed to solve any challenges that may come up. I am confident and calm". Ask your body to release any tension or nervous energy. Then smile and head off to the meeting, feeling centred and prepared. Keep breathing and return to your breath if you feel anxious during the meeting.

Imagine arriving home from work and spending two minutes in your car (or on the bus), doing a transition meditation before you go into the house.

Take 10 deep breaths, thank your mind and your body for supporting you all day. Acknowledge the day is not over, but you are excited to see your family again after such a long and busy day. Calm your mind, let go of stress and tension and feel any sensations that rise up in your body and thank them for the message in helping you be all you need to be in the hours ahead.

Transition meditations are really beneficial when used both frequently or infrequently and are a great resource to call on when needed.

For a free copy of my ebook *Managing Transitions for Parents* please email thewellnesspoet@gmail.com and I will send you a copy.

There are many useful and healing ways to use meditation if you practise regularly. You can train your mind to help you with all kinds of things, from solving problems, to making big decisions, healing your body and creating the future you desire. There are so many great examples of this, and if you want to do more research for yourself, check out work by Dr Joe Dispenza, Bob Proctor, Tara Brach or Deepak Chopra.

I often meditate when I need to make a big decision, because it's a fairly well-known fact that if we make decisions when stressed, we are more likely to regret it or make a mistake. We are actually 40% dumber when we are stressed. Avoiding making decisions under stress and pressure is sometimes difficult, however the reality is if we can manage our stress through managing our thoughts, feelings and emotions, then we are more likely to make healthy decisions.

Meditation helps us control our stress, thoughts, feelings and emotions. This makes our decision-making more focused, as we are less stressed and in touch with our inner self (or intuition). The wise old saying, "follow your heart" is incredibly apt because our heart radiates a frequency of up to three feet outside of our body, whereas our brain radiates a frequency of up to 30cm outside of our head. So, following our heart and trusting our gut (if we quieten our mind), is going to lead to choices that sit more comfortably with our soul.

If you are faced with difficult emotions or have personal conflict with someone, you can try to understand why you may be feeling a certain way about this thing in your life. You can practise a meditation that encourages you to let go of hurt feelings and emotions. You may notice a sick feeling in your solar plexus or stomach when you have conflict or upset in your life and this is completely normal.

If this happens, you can say to your body, "I acknowledge I am experiencing some pain and I'm not sure why I'm feeling like this". From my experience, by acknowledging these emotions frequently during the time you are having them and not asking for the answer, the answer will appear to you in a moment of quiet.

An example is that you've been spending time with someone who is very negative about life or even abusive and they make you feel hurt, frustrated, resentful and upset inside. As soon as you notice you are feeling like this, you can acknowledge the feelings. "I'm feeling hurt/resentful/angry/sad and I'm not sure why exactly, but I trust that there is a message here for me and it will come to me when I'm ready to accept it." Usually the message will come to you within hours or a few days if you keep asking the question and acknowledging the feeling. The answer could be:

- Spending time with negative people is very draining and makes you become negative in your thoughts and you would rather not expose yourself to so much negativity. Their comments or beliefs may be in conflict with your values and this does not sit well with you.

- The toxic or abusive person has caused you pain and suffering and spending time with them causes you to remember the abuse. You need to let go of your suffering, accept it for what it was and thank them for the lessons you learned. Know that you are a strong, kind and compassionate person and forgive them for their mistakes as they are suffering too.

- You didn't handle a situation with a friend or family member well and you feel guilty or annoyed that you showed a side of yourself that you would rather they had not seen. You can acknowledge that by holding onto these feelings, you are extending your suffering, you will try not to repeat the suffering next time and you give yourself permission to let go of any hurt you caused the person and forgive yourself. You can apologise to yourself and if possible, them as well, when you feel it's right to do so.

There are literally dozens of meditation apps and hundreds of hours of free meditations on YouTube. In the early days of this step, look for ones that are 10–12 minutes long focused on reducing stress, tension, anxiety, letting go, calming your mind and breathing. As you become more comfortable with the process, you can expand your learning by extending the duration and meditating on themes that are important to you. For example, letting go of negativity, creating positive thoughts, building love and intimacy, manifesting abundance, raising your frequency, healing past abuses and hurts, cord cutting, self-acceptance and self-love, and so on.

Yoga is great not just for the benefits of stretching, but developing body and breath awareness: a fundamental skill of meditation. There are many forms of yoga, and if you haven't done it before, going to your first yoga class is a big step. But let me tell you a secret, yoga is just stretching in different shapes and forms and if you did PE in school or played sport, chances are you did some form of stretching. You can find many simple yoga sequences on YouTube to follow that will allow you to practise at home until you feel comfortable taking some classes. Thirty minutes of stretching and breathing each evening before bed, either before or after a 10-minute meditation, is an amazing wind down at the end of a long day and will help bring your body back to homeostasis and prepare it for a night of rest and repair.

Regular yoga practice has so many benefits for you physically and mentally. I strongly encourage you to at least try some free community classes where the expectation for you to reach your toes and stand on your head is not so high. Yoga should be practised at your own pace and within your limits. A good yoga teacher will provide you with the guidance and support that is right for you.

At the end of this step, you will set an intention to incorporate meditation as part of your life to enable you to ride life's exciting roller-coaster with a calm, centred, thoughtful curiosity and wonder!

Step 5 Recap

1. Meditate for 10-12 minutes each day.

2. Practise transition meditations throughout your day.

3. Stretch, stretch and stretch.

4. Notice how you are feeling throughout your day and rather than judge your feelings be curious about them.

5. Direct loving kindness towards yourself and others.

"The thing about meditation; you become more and more you."

\- David Lynch

"Just one small positive thought in the morning can change your whole day."

\- Dalai Lama

"Every breath is a meditation if you focus your attention on it."

\- Eckhart Tolle

Peace

There's a piece of me, that craves some peace from me,
All the thinking, all the blinking, a feeling that I'm sinking.
The busyness, the craziness, the tiredness, the laziness,
The expectations not met, all the feelings of regret.

The jumpiness, the bossiness, trying to mind my own business,
The over-functioning desire, to fix, to help, to enquire.
To plan, to do, to make, it's all just one big mistake,
I'm done, I need a break.

I got my wake-up call, it took a while that's all,
To find the missing piece, which enabled stillness and peace.
I found the key, to a vault inside of me,
Where all this noise was going on, not helpful but not wrong.
I cleaned it up, dusted it out, told that negative self-talk to
move on out.
I got my peace, I got my quiet, for now, I've calmed the riot!

:JOY:

STEP 6

Joy

A lot has been written about joy recently and discussions held about the difference between joy and happiness. For me, joy was not something I had ever spent any time contemplating and, looking back now, I don't remember acknowledging joy at any point in my life. I had moments of sheer elation and extreme happiness, but I did not recognise them as joy.

Joy seems to be a very popular word these days, so I thought to myself, "What's all this talk about joy? Why is joy some new self-help buzzword that experts tell us we can't live without?". In fact, many First World countries are now looking at the happiness of their inhabitants as a measure of success or failure!

In Step 6 you will devote 30 days to thinking about joy, to understand it, to acknowledge it, to research it and to share it as much as you can.

Here's what I've learned about joy and why you should embrace it as Step 6 to an unbreakable you.

Happiness is temporary and comes and goes with events in our day or our life. Joy is innate and inside all of us, and it's only when you are present in the moment and feel connected to the world around you, that you experience joy. We can often overlook joy because we are waiting for the happy moments. When life becomes busy and stressful and we have heartaches and setbacks, noticing and experiencing joy can be the furthest thing from our mind.

However, we can get back to joy anytime we want to, and we should regularly take time to notice joy and experience it, regardless of how unhappy our circumstances may be at the time.

I researched a lot of articles about joy and noted that even Jesus preached about joy to his followers. You don't have to be a Christian to have a sense of wonder and openness about joy. Living life with a focus on joy, puts things into a whole new perspective.

If you've suffered hardships, abuse, grief, loss, trauma, depression, addiction, low self-esteem, then joy is probably not something you turned to in order to heal your wounds. Surprisingly, I have found, and since learned, that joy is one of the best healers. It is within all of us to feel joy, just as the emotional and mental suffering we endure is within all of us.

Here are some practical ways you can find joy, feel joy and spread joy, which will have a huge impact on your life and wellbeing. You can practise all of them over the next 30 days:

1. Write down your own definition of joy, this becomes your line in the sand to which you understand joy.

2. Read about joy. You only have to type the word joy into your browser and a wealth of information and interesting views about joy are told in fascinating and eye-opening ways. You may even want to go back and review your definition.

3. Meditate on joy – there are many free meditations on YouTube that focus on joy.

4. Sit or walk in nature and let your soul connect with the other living things around you. You will start to notice a deeper sense of connection which builds internal contentment and peace.

5. When you notice something that you find joyful, or you feel true joy, acknowledge it and thank it for being in your life.

6. Connect to your breath several times throughout the day and look outside and appreciate the joy of being alive. No-one can take away from you the simple pleasure of breathing in and out and thanking the universe for all your blessings and the joy that surrounds you.

7. Write down five things that bring you true joy.

8. If you have children, you may want to talk about the joy they bring you.

9. When you are relaxing, close your eyes and visualise the most joyous moment in your life and then smile to yourself.

10. If something makes you feel joyous, tell people about it and don't be afraid to sound corny. Sometimes describing a simple, joyous moment sounds corny when you say it out loud, but you are reinforcing that moment in your DNA, and you will have no trouble finding that joy again.

11. If a person makes you feel joy, share it with them as soon as you can – preferably right in the moment. Don't be afraid to put all your words and emotion into explaining why they brought you joy and how you wish that this moment will stay with you forever.

12. Set some time aside each month just to think about how you can bring joy to other people through your words, actions or behaviours and remember to acknowledge those moments when they come up.

If you set an intention to notice and feel joy, you will have a deeper connection with yourself and the world around you. Radiating joy from your heart will impact anyone that comes within three feet of you, according to epigenetics, and that's a pretty special way to go about your day. Even when you are having a less than smooth day yourself, you will have a positive effect on someone else.

J – **Just**
O – **Open**
Y – **Yourself**

Now, some of you may be sitting there and thinking, "That's all very well for you, you may not have experienced the same kind of hardships as me, so all this talk about joy is a luxury". I probably thought that too when I first set the intention to have joy. I have faced sadness and losses and read a lot of stories of people who have suffered more than I, and they too, had the capacity to recognise and feel joy even in the most desperate of human conditions.

Getting in touch with your innate joy will bring you peace and harmony. It will help you to appreciate the wonderous moments in life and to take a big breath and suck up all that joy and then share it with others. Joy shared, is not joy halved. Joy shared multiplies like a virus and infects people on a cellular level, and that is not only good for you, but all living things around you. Spread the joy my friends!

By now, you have been through Steps 1–6, which I call the "Soft Stuff". You may have looked at those steps and thought, "That's easy, what's the big deal, I'm just not looking forward to Step 7!"

Steps 1–6 are your foundation, your bedrock to your unbreakable mind and spirit. If you commit to them, set your intentions, practise and review your work daily and accumulatively, you will be on a path to transformation. Soft skills are often the hardest to teach and people learn the slowest. In my experience, the soft skills are where the "wow" moments come from. The skills that allow us to impress ourselves and others with our care, attention, thoughtfulness, love, gratitude, and leave us wanting more. The priceless moments.

The funny thing is, we spend so little of our time and attention on growing and developing our soft skills. We make excuses – "Oh, that's just how I am!". Like learning to ride a bike, use an iPhone or any other skill, we can learn and develop our soft skills on an ongoing basis, we can trade them, upgrade them and keep people wanting more of us!

From Step 7 onwards we focus on building up our body and move into our learning and growth zone. There will be further insights, learnings and motivation. It's important not to do Steps 1–6 in half measures, because you won't be able to embrace the full benefits of Steps 7–12, and you won't be opening yourself up to a whole new world of thinking and living.

And remember, as we move forward into the remaining steps, you are continuing to practise the previous steps on a regular basis. They have become a part of your lifestyle and your healthy habits. You can check in with yourself every week or so:

1. Have I written in my journal lately?
2. Have I filed my feelings, thoughts, bills, paperwork and decluttered some parts of my home?
3. Have I used mindfulness in all areas of my life: work, home, relationships and practised meditation regularly?
4. Have I appreciated all that is good in my life, thanked my life for all the lessons it has given me and been grateful for the opportunities that I have ahead of me?
5. Have I noticed joy, expressed joy, talked about joy and shared joy with myself and others?
6. Am I ready to embark on the remaining six steps? Absofreakinlootely!

If you are a person that likes to get ahead on your projects (like me), you were already probably thinking about Step 7 and beyond, and you may have already taken some actions and set some intentions because you knew what was coming. If you didn't do this, that's OK too, because we all need to work at our own pace and these steps are not a race with anyone. The fundamental thing is to build your own foundation. My steps are a guide to help direct you, inform you and inspire you.

The "soft stuff" in Steps 1–6 at times may have felt really heavy and deep, but you have to do the inner work before you can do the outer work. You then have the opportunity to design your own future. We neglect our inner world so often and then wonder why our outer world is in total chaos and we have so many aches and pains in our body and our life.

Bringing our bodies back to homeostasis is fundamental for repair, regrowth, rebuilding and regenerating both internally and externally.

As you move forward, revisit your journal regularly and any lessons in this book that have been insightful to you personally. I expect by now your thirst for knowledge is starting to increase and you've started watching, listening and reading content you've not engaged with either for a long time or ever before. You've made space for new stuff. Well done, keep going!

Step 6 Recap

1. Notice moments of joy and really feel them and then talk about them.

2. Joy is innate in all of us and our soul is fed from joy. Nourish your soul with joy.

3. Develop your soft skills, impress yourself and others with your care, attention, thoughtfulness, love, gratitude and leave people wanting more.

4. Connect to your breath several times throughout the day and notice nature.

5. Meditate on joy.

"Without pain, how could we know joy?"
- Unknown

"When you do things from your soul, you feel a river moving in you, a joy."
- Rumi

What the Heck is Joy

What the heck is joy?
It's been playing on my mind,
It's like some forbidden toy,
I just can't seem to find.
I've written it down,
Mulled over it a bit,
This illustrious crown,
It doesn't quite fit.
Somewhere deep inside I know it must be,
But surely it isn't just me,
That thinks this joy is some kind of lark,
Not the hallowed ground away from the dark.
Maybe it's just joy doesn't feel normal,
I'm used to feeling things a bit more formal.
This word joy is being tossed around,
Online, in circles, in books I have found.
I don't think life is so simple,
As a 3-letter word that can spread like a dimple,
On our face, in our heart, in the deepest part,
Of our body, our mind of the ethereal kind.
What is this joy, I have to ask?
Can I get some, do I have to fast?
I'm waiting in line, I'm waiting my turn,
Perhaps it's something, I have to earn.
One day there will be a knock at my door,
That joy will arrive and go straight to the core.
I'll care for it and watch it thrive,
I'll spread that joy, far and wide,
For joy is something you cannot hide.
It's kindness, it's love, it's being at peace,
It ebbs and it flows to say the least.
3 little letters,
That's JOY and it matters.

@thewellnesspoet 🅕 🅞 @thewellnesspoet1

STEP 7

Jogging

I know what you are thinking, I've heard it all before: the objections, the excuses, the doubts, the injuries, the time, the knees, the hips, the heart, you name it – I've heard it. So, I'm going to share some stories and then you can reassess your mindset! Then, I'm going to offer up some options and you can embrace Step 7 for the next 30 days.

Now, just a note, you don't need to jog every day for 30 days. If you haven't jogged in many years/decades/months or even weeks, then take it slow. Set an intention to move your body: walk – stretch – jog – walk – stretch.

The aim of Step 7 is to embrace movement into your life on a daily basis.

As a society, unfortunately, we have become far too sedentary. We sit for long periods every day and then come home and sit down to eat, watch TV and then lay down and sleep. Our daily movement is very limited, and for many of us, we spend far too much time in our cars and on public transport.

Most of us generally do know that we need to exercise to lose weight and stay healthy, but the reality is that exercise has far greater reaching benefits than we all probably appreciate.

Here's the top 10 exercise benefits for your mind, body and spirit:

1. Exercise increases your energy levels.
2. Exercise reduces your risk of chronic disease.
3. Exercise lowers your biological age.
4. Exercise makes you feel happier and improves your mood.
5. Exercise helps you lose weight and maintain a healthy BMI.
6. Exercise improves circulation which helps your brain health and memory.
7. Exercise helps build and maintain strong bones and muscles.

8. Exercise helps us sleep better.
9. Exercise helps reduce pain and aids with pain management.
10. Exercise improves hair and skin by improving surface blood circulation and taking away cell debris.

Interestingly, high-impact sports, such as jogging, soccer or basketball, have been shown to promote higher bone density than non-impact sports like swimming or cycling. Jogging will help build bone density and prevent osteoporosis in later life.

Many of us feel mentally fatigued at the end of a long day or after a rough night, so the idea of getting up early or exercising in the evening just isn't a priority.

There is a big difference though between mental and physical fatigue, and it's very important to recognise that if we are sitting down all day then we are not physically fatigued.

Exercise has been shown to improve conditions like chronic fatigue, multiple sclerosis and progressive illnesses, such as cancer and AIDS, because exercise helps us build new cells. Regular exercise of up to 75 minutes per week has proven to reduce the risk of heart disease and diabetes. Another little-known fact about exercise is that it can actually help reduce chronic pain.

We've generally been told to rest and be inactive when we have pain, however, more recent studies show that exercise actually helps relieve chronic pain. Many of us suffer with some sort of pain due to modern life and our largely sedentary lifestyle. If we are not sitting at a desk all day, we are in our cars, on public transport or sitting at home.

The key is to exercise and stretch. By stretching our bodies, we aid in the repair of our body and by exercising we stimulate the blood flow and send nutrients to cells that need repairing.

So why is Step 7 so crucial?

The World Health Organization says that, *"18–64 year olds should do at least 150 minutes of moderate-intense aerobic physical activity, or at least 75 minutes of vigorous-intensity aerobic physical activity throughout the week, which should be performed for at least 10 minutes in duration at a minimum".*

So that could equate to 3 x 25-minute jogs per week of approximately 3–5kms depending on your speed. Can you do that?

In addition, the World Health Organization states there is strong evidence to demonstrate that men and women who are more active have lower rates of heart disease, high blood pressure, type 2 diabetes, colon and breast cancer and depression. Many of these illnesses are related to what we put into our bodies and what we don't put out.

Here's some tips to get you jogging again, which you can do over the next 30 days and beyond. If you are focused, you should notice that in 5–6 weeks you can jog 3–4kms without stopping.

1. Walk 30–60mins, 3 x per week at a varied pace.
2. Stretch daily 20–30mins whilst practising breathing.
    ➢ Deep belly breaths – breathe in for four, hold for four, breathe out for four.
3. Take daily supplements that support gut health, muscle function, joints and prevent inflammation (magnesium, probiotics, glucosamine and turmeric).
4. Hill walking if you have one nearby to improve cardio fitness (60–90mins, once per week).
5. Yoga classes to improve flexibility (1–2 times per week).
6. Slow jogging 1km.
7. Increase plant-based foods in your diet, including kale, quinoa, nuts and seeds.
8. Repeat all steps above continuously then build up to slow jogging 2km.

9. Epsom salts/magnesium baths 1–2 x week or as needed.
10. Switch driving/public transport with walking 1–2 x week (to work, to shops, to school).
    ➢ Park further away and walk, or get off a few stops early and walk the rest.
    ➢ Take the stairs not the lift or escalator.

How do I know this works? Because as a middle-aged woman, I was overweight with breast cysts, constant soft tissue pain, mild depression and mood swings, low energy, weak hair, congested and mottled skin. After six months of jogging all of these were gone. My biological age had improved by up to 10 years and I lost 15kgs.

Of course, the conditions above had not just happened overnight, it was over a long period of time, through different life stages when the focus on being young and active and having fun shifted to being serious, having a career, making money, trying to make a baby and becoming a mum. There were times throughout when I had a health kick, took up Yoga again, lost weight, etc., but it was not sustained as every time work got busy or I travelled, it unravelled quite quickly.

Over a decade I had become far too sedentary in my work and social life. I had far too much refined carbohydrates, sugar, alcohol, meat and dairy in my diet, which I traded for plant-based substitutes or just cut out altogether. After completing Steps 1–6, I was in a totally different frame of mind and it is imperative to me that my body be healthy so that I can achieve my goal (end date 2083).

After researching and understanding the actual broader benefits of exercise (not just for getting fit), I was making it my priority to move my body, do some jogging and take care of myself physically.

To start jogging again after 20 years with all of the health conditions I had would undoubtedly be hard. I was under no illusion, but I decided I would do it for FUN! Yes, fun! I would embrace jogging as my fun thing to do in order to find my youth and vitality once again. I had suffered sciatica during my pregnancies and since I'd been sedentary for much of the past decade, my knees were not that excited about jogging either. I followed my 10 tips above and in no time I was enjoying my jogging, relatively pain free and seeing great benefits to my health and overall wellbeing. I even did some local running festivals just for fun!

The aim of Step 7 is to educate you on the long-term benefits of exercise and to encourage you to choose it as priority. Keep it high on your list of priorities each day, so that you can live a healthier, happier, longer life. And if you need any reminders, drive by your local hospital at 2pm on a Tuesday and see all the sick people going for treatment and then decide whether you would rather spend 30 minutes 3 x per week exercising, rather than hours in a hospital waiting room to see a doctor about an illness related to poor diet and lack of exercise. Don't waste your life in a hospital, go for a walk or a jog instead.

Now, I did promise some other options for those who are against jogging or have had knees and hips replaced. Note: exercise and stretching will help improve bad knees and hips, and taking glucosamine and turmeric will help repair your joint cartilage and reduce inflammation.

1. If you can't bring yourself to jog then brisk **Walking** will do, if you do it a few times per week.

2. You could try **Jumping** on a trampoline. Ten minutes of jumping on a trampoline burns a lot of calories, is fun, will help your pelvic floor and you can do it with your kids.

3. You could try a **Judo** class! Why not learn some self-defence, meet new people and get fit and stronger in the process?

4. Play **Jianzi** in the backyard with your family. Jianzi is a traditional Chinese sport, where you aim to keep a shuttlecock in the air using your feet and legs only. It's also called Shuttlecock and is great fun to do at home or in the park with your friends.

5. Learn to **Jive**, it's a great way to meet people, have fun and burn calories. You can learn with friends and family and swing your way round the house!

The aim is to move: move well, move regularly and keep moving all through the day. Notice when you've been sitting down for too long, get up and move. Don't seek the sofa, seek your sneakers and hit the pavement.

If you are wheelchair bound or have lost limbs then lower body movement may not be possible. I know very well these challenges, as I've cared for both paraplegics and quadriplegics in my life. My recommendation is to take regular physical therapy, both assisted and unassisted, in order to keep your joints supple and promote freedom of movement and to prevent total muscle atrophy.

There are a whole range of physical therapy and movement-based activities for those with disabilities. Avoiding it is not an option if you want to be healthy throughout your life. Taking an active mental approach to activity, even with a disability, will promote the benefits listed above.

Earlier I mentioned that we often mistake mental fatigue with physical fatigue. It's important to understand and address the impacts of mental fatigue so that you don't cause yourself further harm by not doing physical activity.

Mental fatigue is defined as: a condition triggered by prolonged cognitive activity. The most common symptoms include mental block, lack of motivation, irritability, stress eating or loss of appetite, and insomnia.

Now interestingly, if you remember earlier in this step, physical exercise was shown to improve all the symptoms caused by mental fatigue. So, the best cure for a long busy day at the office or stuck at home all day is to get out and exercise. Of course, your brain is going to tell you that you are too tired, too busy, it's too late, and that you need to eat and go to bed and relax on the sofa. We make unhealthy choices when we are mentally fatigued, in the same way we make unhealthy choices when we are stressed.

Don't let your mental fatigue dictate your physical health. You can take control of that voice in your head when an objection comes up.

"Thank you for the message, I know you are tired but my body needs to move now, so just relax and enjoy the increased blood flow, endorphins and change of scenery!"

Then just put your shoes on AND GO!

Some bodies wear out earlier than others, and sometimes we get injured or have a medical condition that prevents us doing what we would ideally love to do. What I also see is people who make lots of excuses for themselves, because they know that high-intensity exercise is quite challenging and sometimes painful in the beginning, particularly when you are unfit, overweight or in an emotional funk. It takes a lot of work to get fit and stay fit. But the great part about walking and jogging is other than clothes and shoes it is free. You can do it anywhere and you can take people with you.

I studied Mechanisms and Management of Injuries at university and represented Australia in sport at an international level, and then became an overweight, sedentary, middle-aged woman (or a fat middle-aged exec as I fondly called myself). I'm all too aware of the aches, the pains, the excuses, the challenges and the uncomfortable feelings and embarrassment of taking up jogging again.

On one particular day in the early stages of jogging, some teenage boys were making fun of me. Mimicking my running, blustering and facial expressions. I was embarrassed, humiliated, and angry. How dare those pimple-face brats make fun of me, don't they know what I've been through and how hard this is?

"No, they don't!"

And that's what I kept telling myself as I continued running. I may have been someone to laugh at to them, but to me, I was overcoming years of pain and suffering, one step at a time.

A few months into my jogging a lady older than me commented that my stretching looked painful. I was doing a hip stretch on a park bench and it is uncomfortable, but it's amazing for your hips.

She said, *"Oh, that looks painful!"* as she walked past.

I quipped back, *"Not as painful as it is if you don't do it!"*

We both laughed, she said, *"Yes, that's true!"*

Things that are good for us are not easy or comfortable, just like saving money, going for a promotion or having children. We put exercise and stretching in the too-hard basket while we take on much bigger challenges in our life. This seems strange to me now!

Don't let anyone fool you into thinking that you are not good enough to go jogging, take up jogging or ever jog in an organised event. You just have to turn up! When you turn up you give yourself permission to try. Just have fun and laugh at yourself. In 6–12 months, with regular jogging all your doubters and haters will be laughing on the other side of their face as your physical health goes from broken to unbreakable.

If you find yourself injured or in pain, have a magnesium bath, do lots of stretching, get some arnica and magnesium cream, take some turmeric and be kind to yourself. In a few days you will feel better again and you can just start where you left off. You are only doing this for yourself. I had a very memorable few days where my inner thighs shouted at me in pain: *"What the hell are you doing you silly old cow, stop running!"* I rubbed them, stretched them, thanked them and carried on. They never shouted at me again.

Now, if you already know all of this, you exercise and jog regularly, well done! You are flying through Step 7. Do consider daily stretching, yoga and the supplements mentioned above if you've not had them before, because you want to protect yourself 30–40 years in the future. How nimble, flexible and pain free do you want to be? Safeguard yourself now for problems that can and do arise later in life.

Sadly, I see so many people who do jog that don't stretch and don't take any supplements, and in their middle age they have the common problems; hip, knee, back pain and foot pain. Protect your joints, your feet, your hips and back and take preventative steps that repair and promote the health of your body. This is the best way to have an active, longer life.

What most of us don't realise is that sitting in a fixed position at a desk, or working in a fixed position all day, such as a roofer, tiler or mechanic, you are doing your body damage. At the end of a long day of work you need to stretch out those muscles that you have been using. Stretching is not just for after jogging, it's after work, after sitting, after bending, after driving long hours. Your hip flexors become so tight from sitting or bending over all day that you will find hip and back pain is never far away.

Setting the intention to jog is the first step to achieving it and I tell everyone:

"If I can do it, you can do it!"

Just start with setting the intention, take action and share your results, even if you just log them initially to keep track. When you become more confident in yourself you can share your results, photos, or funny stories that happen when you jog. You will meet other joggers and have funny moments; you will get caught in the rain or fall on your face. But with each forward step you are propelling yourself to a healthier, happier life, and that is what Step 7 is all about.

Reminder – always wear sun cream!

Step 7 Recap

1. Set an intention to move your body daily – Jog, Walk, Jump, Jive!

2. Use physical activity to help with mental fatigue.

3. We build new cells and repair our bodies when we exercise.

4. We prevent chronic illnesses and disease through vigorous exercise 3 x per week.

5. Exercise improves memory and aids in longevity.

"Don't seek the sofa, seek your sneakers and hit the pavement not the wall."
- The Wellness Poet

"If it doesn't challenge you, it won't change you!"
- Fred Devito

"Running is mind over matter. If your head doesn't mind, your body doesn't matter!"
- Ultra Running Quote

"Running reminds you that even in your weakest moments, you are strong!"
- Run-for-good.com

Ode to parkrun

It started with a joke and a walk,
An aching body and negative self-talk,
Now watch me go, I'm not so slow,
I've 20 runs in the bank and sub 27 minutes in the tank.

It's the friendly faces and speedy racers,
Old folk, young folk, no joke,
All running with joy and careless abandon,
A lot of laughter and a kick of adrenalin.

Watch out for the magpie that swoops and the dogs that poop,
And enjoy the sunrise and bird song, as you go along,
Get your barcode ready and be set at the steady,
And thank the volunteers, who deserve the biggest cheers.

For me, it's the spirit and a little bit of fun,
Fresh air, water views and the morning sun,
So, get yourself down to your nearest one,
5ks every Saturday, that is parkrun!

@thewellnesspoet @thewellnesspoet1

STEP 8

Adventure

To stand at the top of a mountain, deep in a rainforest, or on the moon, lost in the vastness of it all may be an adventure that many of us would never dare to attempt. Explorers and adventurers have a spirit and determination that guides them to push themselves to their outer limit in order to see what is there. Without them, we would not have the discoveries or territories we have today. Our possibilities are endless! Is this you?

On the other hand, many of us like to play it safe and keep within our safe space, familiar territory and close to people we know and trust. For others, everyday life may be an adventure, with the physical, mental and emotional challenges that come up.

The definition of **adventure** is: an unusual and exciting or daring experience. To engage in a daring or risky activity.

Even if you do like to play it safe, the reality is that based on the definition above, we are living an adventure every day. Why? Because we take risks every day with the decisions we make. We also engage in unusual experiences and seek out things that excite us like sport, video games, gambling, drinking, bingeing, shopping, etc.

Some adventures will bring us fulfilment, joy and wonder. Others will bring us debt, addiction, weight gain and suffering.

In Step 8, we are going to practise healthy adventure seeking. This means we are going to seek out opportunities to grow, to learn, to develop, to wonder and to experience unusual things that benefit our health and wellbeing.

It might sound strange that this is necessary, but if you embrace this idea and you open yourself up to adventure, in whatever form it presents itself, you are opening up to a whole new world of opportunities. This includes self-discovery and self-expression, and what could be more adventurous than that?

It's important to understand and consider that an adventure for you is different for me, as our inner and outer limits are all different – and that's okay!

In setting the intention to seek adventure for 30 days, I was trusting that whatever adventures presented themselves to me, I would embark upon them, knowing that they were the right ones for me. If they were healthy, contributed to my personal development and allowed me to continue to practise all of the previous steps, then I would embrace them.

When we "play it safe", it's because we have become used to living in our comfort zone, which is a familiar space, where we feel in control of things around us. As adults, we probably spend a lot of time in our comfort zone because we had many years outside of it, dealing with school, college, training, becoming a parent for the first time, etc. It can be natural to want life to feel "safe" and to be "in control", after all isn't that what adulting is – being in control?

The challenge with spending too much time or too long in our comfort zone is that we stagnate as individuals and end up becoming sheep-like creatures of habit that do what we like to do. If we step outside our comfort zone, we tip into the void. This is our fear zone since we don't know what's out there. We may bump into judgemental people and then lack confidence to do what we want to do. That's kind of scary, so best just to go back to the comfort zone until things feel right. But when do things feel right?

When is it the right time to step out of our comfy slippers, put on our hiking boots and head for the hills? I mean that figuratively, not literally. Well, now is the right time. You've noted that you are living in your comfort zone most of the time, you've noted that you might have stagnated, become a bit judgemental yourself and that if you stay here you are missing a whole world of potential.

So, get your boots on, we are going for a walk!

Let's look at an example of healthy adventure seeking:

- You would like to try some new things, learn some new things or undertake some personal development.
- You've already mastered recognising self-doubt and excuses from your mindfulness practice and you've set the intention to go into this with your mind and eyes open for what adventures may come up.
- You are presented with an opportunity to undertake a personal development program that enables you to learn new skills, meet new people, create connections, understand your strengths and weaknesses and provide you with ongoing support for years to come.

   Do you?
   a. Tell yourself now is not the right time?
   b. Talk to your most negative friend about it and then decide it is not for you?
   c. Jump right in and see what comes?

Hopefully you answered C. You jump right in and see what comes. Because most of the fear is just deciding to actually do it in the first place. Making the decision to do something is often the hardest part. Once you decide, you can just get on with doing it, taking the actions, participating, letting it unfold and embracing challenges that might present themselves. Congratulations, you are now in the learning zone. You have crossed the void.

Once you reach your learning zone, you will quickly realise there are loads of adventurous people out there as well. They have done what you want to do and left judgement and self-sabotage behind them. And you know what's amazing about these people? They are the encouragers! The ones that are not going to criticise you or tear you down or undermine your choices. They are the ones who are going to get behind you, help you, lift you up and say: "Hey, good job!".

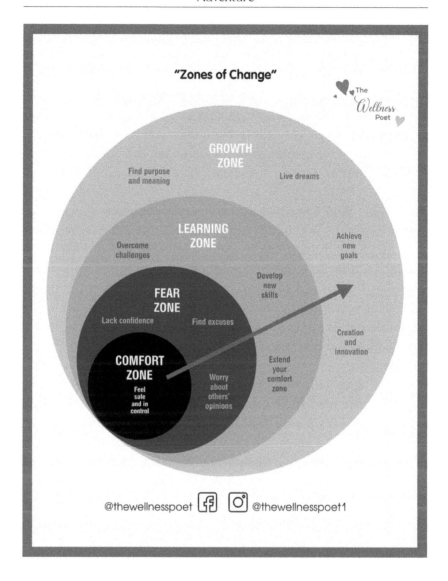

"Zones of Change"

The Wellness Poet

GROWTH ZONE
Find purpose and meaning
Live dreams

LEARNING ZONE
Overcome challenges
Achieve new goals

FEAR ZONE
Develop new skills

Lack confidence
Find excuses

COMFORT ZONE
Feel safe and in control
Worry about others' opinions
Extend your comfort zone
Creation and innovation

@thewellnesspoet @thewellnesspoet1

I know it's hard to imagine that people like this exist, especially in our comfort zone. The other reality of our comfort zone is that the people in this space, are the people that expect the least from you. They are not necessarily the ones hoping you soar to amazing heights, because then they will miss you. They may even miss judging you, holding you back and keeping you down.

Those people in your comfort zone tend to be the ones you love most in the world and that's where life has become a bit messed up. We all do it, we all think we have the right to keep our loved ones in their safe "Comfort Zone" and if they start to do things a bit different, then we judge them, we might try to talk them out of it and we might even put barriers in their way. This is very unfortunate, because all we do is stop the people we love the most reaching their full potential – living their adventure!

In October 2019 I watched a great interview between Trevor Noah and Will Smith. Will Smith had just turned 50 and was struggling with the idea of maintaining his identity and caring about what people thought of him. So much so that he joked for his birthday he should probably do what white people do to celebrate the milestones and go sky diving or something. But instead he decided that on turning 50 he would not be afraid to say what he thought and do whatever the hell he liked and that was real adventure.

I tend to agree with Will, on reaching a certain age and level of life experience we need to be comfortable with who we are and to have confidence to say what we think, even if we know others may not agree with us. There is a lot of talk amongst celebrities and self-help gurus about authenticity and being authentic. It makes sense, because if you are too scared to take an actual position on something, people won't trust you. Like with politicians who sit on the fence. Jeremy Corbyn is a typical example in respect of the UK and Brexit. He did not state clearly his honest position and tried to play both sides. Despite being a hero three years earlier, he fell to zero in the 2019 election, because no-one knew his position or felt that he could be fully trusted to do the right thing.

If you choose a path that is untrodden, a position which is new but you believe in it, or are adventurous enough to say and do what you think, then you are being true to yourself and living authentically. People may leave you during this time, but as long as you are not deliberately hurting others, in the future those that left you may have new respect for you. Those that doubted you or thought you were crazy for walking a new path may now believe in you. You can't wait for others to get on the same path as you. You have to live your life and lead by example, live by the values you hold closest to you and let your soul guide you. This is a very adventurous path.

The hardest part about changing yourself is that generally everything else stays the same. Same family members, same partner, same stressors, same responsibilities. Of course, a mass overhaul of your life is not always possible but even small changes to your lifestyle can be difficult when you are still living and working in the same environment. It takes courage, commitment and consistency because there will be days it will be easier to be the old you, not make a fuss and just continue with your old habits. Being mindful of this will help keep you focused when you feel it's too hard or it's easier just to do what everyone else is doing.

The goal in this step is to move seamlessly from your comfort zone to your growth zone and back again. This can happen throughout your day/week/month on an ongoing basis. It merely means you are not stuck.

The growth zone is where the magic happens, where you reach your full potential. I don't mean a wealthy, megalomaniac. I mean the person who feels whole, in mind, body and spirit, because you have recognised and attended to all the things in your life that needed some work, physically, mentally, emotionally, and on a personal development level. You may not have it all figured out right now, but you are ready for the adventure to figure it out. That adventure will continue once you've acknowledged this and you seek some opportunities to learn and grow.

I will be careful to say that if we focus too heavily on one level of learning it can become a heavy burden or we compromise other areas of our life, such as our health. For instance, if you are very focused on learning and studying, you may invest a lot of your time and energy in that one area to the detriment to your physical health. Whereas if you invest a lot of time in conquering fears through physical challenges, such as marathons or mountain climbing, you may distance yourself from other things in your life.

Finding harmony and balance in life for your mind, body and spirit is an adventure we should all undertake, which involves continual learning, growth and not letting our fears hold us back, whilst we are safe in the knowledge that we can return to our comfort zone for a good rest and some respite whenever we need it.

My adventure started with accepting that I wanted to write, not knowing where to start. I decided I would call myself a 'Writer' and introduce myself as one to new people I met. So, I went along to a Kerwin Rae event and when people asked me what I did, I told them; *"I am a writer!"*

The writing adventure started with writing poems in my journal, followed by publishing them in some groups and then setting up a Facebook page to share my poetry and journey to wellness. This was followed by a website to publish blogs and my poems.

This was quite a big step for me, because my fears and vulnerability were tested big time. I had to overcome my fear of judgement, and fear that I'm not good enough to put my writing out into the world.

The reaction was very positive among new people I met, however for those that have known me longer, the reaction was somewhat mixed. Some just changed the subject or didn't even acknowledge what I said. No encouragement, no words of support, no, *"Good on you, well done!"*, just indifference.

I wondered what they were thinking. Did they think:

"You are not good enough to write a book!"

"Who is going to publish your book?"

"Why would anyone want to buy a book that you have written?"

My overactive imagination and self-doubts allowed me to imagine this is what they were thinking, but they didn't want to say it to me directly. However, here's what I also know. Those people closest to me don't want to see me fail. They also may be nervous about seeing me grow and what if I succeed? This is absolutely normal and you and I probably do it too. We need to accept that it's going to happen, it's a part of life. Those close to us don't want us to have pain and obstacles in our life, but they also don't know your soul like you do, so thank them and carry on anyway.

I decided to put all those doubts, worries and fears to the side and just carry on with my writing and wondering and waiting for opportunities to present themselves. And guess what? I did not need to wait long.

> ➤ I wrote two chapters of my book, attended a publishing workshop, pitched the idea for this book and was offered a publishing contract.
> ➤ I sent my poetry off to five magazines and was picked up and published almost immediately by two of them.

I was a writer, my adventure had begun, and I could now take the bigger step of telling people, *"Yes, I'm writing a book, yes I have a publishing contract, yes my poems are published online and in print, and yes, I love sharing my work on both a micro and macro level."*

How do you start your own adventure?

1. Identify what it is you have always wanted to do, but as yet not done (you may have started and given up, stopped temporarily or had to change direction).
2. Write down your aspiration and your intention: "I desire to be or do XX and I will XX in the next month/year/five years".
3. Start working towards your intention immediately. You don't have to tell people right away, you can just keep it for yourself initially. You will know when is the right time to tell people.
4. Seek out groups of people who have achieved what you would like to achieve and introduce yourself to them. Share your intentions with them to make it real for you. These people will become your support network.
5. Network with those who are doing what you want to do and immerse yourself in the content.
6. Set aside some time each week to practise your intention.
7. Find opportunities to use your skill and share your experience.
8. Know that fears, doubts and obstacles will come up.
9. Practise, practise, practise. Be prepared to fail, failure is part of learning and growth. You can start over as many times as you need, take the lessons and embrace the opportunity to learn new skills.
10. Share your failures, successes, hopes and dreams. The universe wants you to succeed.

Adventures are meant to be fun and challenging, so if you find yourself getting stressed, bored, overwhelmed, or scared, just stop for a bit and remind yourself, "Why did I want to do this? What is my desire and my intention?".

Ask yourself if it is serving you in the way you want it to. The truth is, if it's not, then that's okay too. Nothing (ad)ventured, nothing gained. You can set that one aside and start again, there is no limit to the amount of adventures we get to have in life, that's the amazing part. You may even have some funny stories in the future – "Hey remember that time I did XX, that was hard/hysterical/embarrassing. What was I thinking?!" And you can laugh it off, as long as the cost to you and your loved ones was not too great. I remind you here that I'm referring to healthy adventures, not unhealthy ones!

Adventure seeking, learning and growing can be a very personal and internal thing. It does not have to be physically doing or creating something. A spiritual quest or adventure is just as important as a physical one. Your spiritual health and wellbeing are fundamental to your personal fulfilment, which is why we focused on joy in Step 6. Your adventure should bring you joy.

In moments of hardships, big decisions and life's ups and downs you can ask yourself:

- What will I learn from this?
- How can I grow from this?
- What fears have I overcome as a result of this?

Life is an adventure and embracing the challenges, fears, wonder, worries, doubts and uncertainties is going to allow you to succeed, overcome adversity and gain fulfilment and greater joy in your life. And don't forget, when you see others embarking on their adventure, be an encourager and wish them success.

Open yourself up to adventure for the next 30 days and I promise you amazing opportunities will present themselves, both in the immediate future and down the road. You just have to say yes and not be afraid to fail!

Step 8 Recap

1. Choose your adventure.

2. Understand your "Zones of Change" and what limits you have from spending too much time in your Comfort Zone.

3. Remember that; The hardest part about changing yourself is that generally everything else stays the same.

4. Doubts and fears will come up, that's normal, the best things in life are not easy.

5. Find the support network for your adventure.

"Everyone will underestimate you! The only person who knows the sum of all your parts is you!"

- The Wellness Poet

"Nothing (ad)ventured, nothing gained!"

- The Wellness Poet

A New Comfort Zone

At the edge of the comfortable, lies a great big void,
Full of excuses, fears and a large dose of the paranoid,
But I'm standing at the edge with a mind full of wonder,
Will I jump right in and forget all the blunder?
I've got years of experience to help me plunder,
My mind is made up, I'm not afraid to fail,
I've chart a new course and I'm setting sail,
Straight out of this space known as my comfort zone,
Where new experiences, opportunities and skills I will hone,
I'm ready, I'm steady, I'm raring to go,
Into learning and growth zone, not stopping for No!
I've waited too long at the edge of that void,
But I see now, a new life to be enjoyed!
It stretches, it challenges, it moves at pace,
You can see from a distance the smile on my face,
I'm ready to expand that old comfort zone,
I'm ready to expand and I'm not alone,
I've hit the eject and I've jumped that void,
I'm flying through space like an asteroid,
Those challenges can't stand in my way,
I'll blast them to pieces every day,
I'm ready, I'm set, I've got my cue,
To find a space that's wonderful and new,
It's bigger, it's bolder, it's taking shape,
My comfort zone has a new landscape.

@thewellnesspoet 　 @thewellnesspoet1

STEP 9

Socialising

Social interactions are an important part of life for connectivity and community.

It's easy to get trapped in a social circle, which may include work friends, school friends, university friends, family friends, etc. In this step, we look at the benefits and joys of expanding our social circle and why socialising is important for human nature and growth, as well as healing and support.

The Australian Psychological Society states that in order to thrive, we must have engagement and relationships, as well as positive emotions, accomplishments and meaning, by connecting to something bigger than ourselves.

Whether you find socialising a chore, or you are a social creature who needs interactions with others, setting an intention to socialise is important for three reasons:

1. To build a community of support.
2. To help others and give meaning to your life.
3. To have fun, create positive feelings and laugh.

In Step 9 we are going to commit to finding new ways to be social for 30 days. I don't mean you need to go out for 30 days. If you follow the tips above and start your intention to be social, soon you will find you have a whole new and positive social calendar to look forward to.

In 2020, the global pandemic of the coronavirus cancelled or postponed many social events. Since no-one knows how long the impact will last, it's a very strange time, and as I publish this book, it's probably still ongoing. Community groups and businesses have had to develop new ways to maintain positive social connections due to social distancing, a term we had never heard of until 2020, and we can't forget that many people face financial hardship and lost loved ones. It's hard to feel celebratory or social at a time when people around the world are suffering so greatly as a result of this pandemic.

Finding new and innovative ways to connect and socialise in a positive way is even more important as we are forced into social distancing and isolate ourselves away from our family, friends and colleagues.

Hopefully once this pandemic is over stronger bonds will have been formed in communities and we can start to overcome our collective challenges. This pandemic should also make people acutely aware of their health and prompt them to make healthier choices to prevent risks to themselves and their families.

Even with the pandemic the three reasons to socialise mentioned earlier are very important. You can find ways to achieve them locally in your neighbourhood and globally by sharing your resources, skills and services to help others.

In 2018, I moved home to Australia from the UK and after 15 years living abroad, I didn't know many people when I arrived. I was acutely aware how small my social circle was and that I didn't want to become too needy on those I knew for interaction and stimulation. I needed to find some new herds to be a part of, but ones that gave meaning, joy and fulfilment to my life and were just for me. Not for my kids or my partner.

So, I set some intentions and followed through on them:

1. I engaged in community events, even creating and handing out fliers about a particular issue that was important to me. Most people received it with gratitude, but one woman was immensely rude to me! Uh oh, first social hurdle – time to run home and hide.
   "No, sod her, it's her issue not mine, she is just an angry person who judges others, keep going, you are doing the right thing."

2. I joined a women's networking group and met other women interested in personal growth with a focus on kindness, community and support. Yes, they exist. In a world of negativity, competitive adulting and keeping up with the Joneses, there are groups of women that encourage, support, help and still achieve their own dreams. Find them!

There are men's groups, too. Men who know that vulnerability, compassion, kindness, community and support for each other is the glue that holds us together.

If you can't find either of these groups, then create your own. You only need one like-minded person to start with and you can create a MeetUp.com or informal following where you don't aim to compete, but to share, care and have fun.

Many people relate socialising to drinking alcohol or taking other substances to be more fun. I would encourage you initially to avoid these types of groups. We are aiming for healthy connections that are not based around substances that make you feel down the following day/s.

3. I decided that I would look for opportunities to socialise with new people, which is hard when you have small children. I do believe that we need social circles that don't revolve around our children in order to retain a sense of self and to know ourselves, to understand our wants, needs and desires and to have emotional support for times when we need it from people who know the whole you, not just the parent in you.

There are so many opportunities for social interactions that often we are just too busy to notice. Generally, we are too busy worrying and thinking and we miss the chance to connect with another human right in front of us.

In Step 7 – Jogging, it was not about getting fit, we were jogging for fun (okay, I know jogging is still not fun for some people). The great thing about jogging and walking is you can join community events. A great one, which is worldwide and in many cities all over the world, is called parkrun. I joined parkrun with the aim of jogging and meeting people. During the early days of running, it was hard to talk to people as most of the time I was just focused on breathing with the odd wave. In Step 9, I took the opportunity to be a volunteer at parkrun events and then I started to meet and connect with others in the parkrun community.

I talked, I joked, I laughed, I shared stories, I shared my poetry and I shared my goal of writing a book. I shared my parkrun journey from walker to runner. I met an amazing bunch of talented, helpful and kind individuals and they were all literally on my doorstep every Saturday morning. And best of all, it was free. Running and socialising without spending a cent (penny!).

Connecting in person is so important for positive mental health and wellbeing. Too often we use social media and think we are being 'social'. Taking time away from your device, and sometimes your loved ones, to experience social connections with new people will help you feel more confident, engaged in others, and give you some much needed energy and raise your vibration. You will then attract others who are on the same channel or frequency as you.

Our ego can lead our social interactions and inform our choices, and much of our life is led by our ego. If you've spent time understanding how your ego influences your choices and state of mind then you can ask it to step aside so you have a chance to connect with people who were not worthy of your time before, people who may be different to you. It's those who are different to you that you will learn the most from.

I decided that in order to expand my social network, cultivate meaning in my life and build engagement with my community I would look for opportunities to volunteer in community groups and charities.

Once I set this intention and took a few actions, it did not take long for me to attract the groups that offered me fulfilment, a sense of self-worth and an opportunity to help and add value to others. In fact, two amazing opportunities presented themselves in the same week and as I was already set for whatever adventures came my way, I said yes with only two seconds of hesitation.

Of course, there were people who said, "Oh, wow, you are going to be busy!" but I don't feel that because I chose these opportunities and I enjoy them. They don't feel like chores, they feel like an extension of my passions and interests and have helped me extend my social circle and support network. Now I can give support to others and receive support in equal measure. It's win-win and it's free. I give my time for free and I get back enormous amounts of social engagement for free.

So how do you go about finding social engagements that are right for you?

1. Write down in your journal what inspires you.
2. Write down who inspires you.
3. Write down what and who you find motivating.
4. Write down who and where you can help others.
5. Set an intention to find opportunities to be social and then be open to whatever presents itself.
6. Ignore doubts, criticisms, fears and other people's opinions of what you should be doing.
7. Go out and try new groups, be welcoming, friendly, kind and non-judgemental to others.
8. Share your experiences and vulnerabilities when you feel safe to do so.
9. Leave your ego at home.
10. Leave people with a feeling of "increase" after you've gone home.

What does leaving people with a feeling of "increase" mean?

"Basically, it means that people feel as though you have had a positive impact on them personally, socially, professionally and that because they spent time with you their soul feels bigger. You lifted them up, increased their wellbeing and their spirit!"

I'm very mindful that social anxiety is a recognised medical condition, and from time to time we all suffer from it. Being shy is also an obstacle to engaging in social activities, but in this book, we are 'starting over', so we have a chance to try again and to realise the joys and benefits of socialisation.

According to the Social Anxiety Association, social anxiety is defined as follows: **Social anxiety** is the fear of social situations that involve interaction with other people. You could say social anxiety is the fear and anxiety of being negatively judged and evaluated by other people. It is a pervasive disorder and causes anxiety and fear in most areas of a person's life.

If you suffer from social anxiety, then of course I encourage you to seek some professional help to overcome you worries and fears. If you are in a rut, new to an area or bored with the same talk and people, then seeking new social encounters will open up your life again.

Getting out there after years of moving in the same circles or living in your comfort zone is tough. The hardest part is turning up, especially on your own. You may feel more comfortable taking a friend along the first time. It doesn't matter if you never go with them again, but do keep going. It will take you a very short space of time to find a connection with another person.

The **Wellness** Poet

"I constantly worry what other people may be thinking of me!"

I DON'T HATE YOU, I HAVE A SOCIAL ANXIETY!

@thewellnesspoet @thewellnesspoet1

In a push to leave my own ego at home when I attended events, I set myself a challenge of talking to the first person I happened to stand next to and just say "Hi". At an event I attended, I asked a woman why she was standing in this particular queue and she said she didn't know, she was just standing there because other people were. I told her my motto in life is never stand in line if you don't know where the line is headed. Always walk to the front of the line and ask, "What is this line for?" Then decide if you want to join it.

We laughed and started talking. Turns out she is the owner of a magazine. I told her I was a writer and we became friends almost immediately. I wrote a poem for her magazine, she created a poetry competition for her readers and I became the judge of a nation-wide poetry competition. Amazing! Just because I decided to go to an event, talk to the first person I stood beside and expand my social connections. My desire to be a writer was very quickly realised.

Positive energy attracts positive energy. Negative energy attracts negative energy. If you put out negative energy, vibes, intentions, emotions, thoughts, words and feelings, you will attract the same back. And the opposite is true. If you put out positive thoughts, feelings, emotions, intentions, good vibes, uplifting comments and compliments, you will get back the same in return. Which would you rather, because the reality is that both influence your social circle? If you are a negative person, you will have negative people around you, or possibly no-one. If you are a positive person, you will attract positive people who will lift you up not drag you down.

In some areas of your life, you may actually have both. Recognising this and being prepared to make some changes and difficult choices can be hard. Letting go of negativity and negative people in our life takes work, patience and forgiveness. Only you can make that decision for yourself. By setting an intention to surround yourself with positive and uplifting people, you will soon start to attract and gravitate towards those people. This means you automatically will have less time for those who are negative. The benefits to your health, wellbeing and your emotions can't be measured, but you will feel it in all parts of you.

Stepping away from unhelpful social circles and negative people and influences can take time and sensitivity as you don't want to go out of your way to be hurtful to those you are trying to step away from. Just be mindful that at some point the negativity in them is what attracted you to them in the first place as it mirrored the negativity in you. Noticing and being aware of your own negative thoughts, feelings and emotions and even biases, is key to growth and creating healthy, positive social connections.

If you experience a lot of conflict in your life, you can be curious about that. Generally, conflict arises within us from unhealed wounds from long ago and then manifests in our current relationships. Coming to terms with conflict and understanding the root cause of your conflict will help heal your wounds and give you more positive relationships. Role modelling the behaviours you want to see in others will demonstrate to those who cause you hurt and conflict that you are not going to engage in negative and toxic exchanges or relationships.

It may be a good time now to recap on boundaries! What the heck are boundaries? Believe me, I didn't know either. I decided to be curious about boundaries and think about where my fences may be broken. My life was one big open Serengeti.

Boundaries are invisible barriers you can construct at home, work, with friends, family, lovers, children, etc. They demonstrate to people the ground rules for your relationship. If you've never had them before, your relationships could be a bit volatile or you may be just plain exhausted and worn out of over-giving.

Mark Manson, who wrote *Everything is F*cked – a Book about Hope* has a very insightful blog about boundaries: https://markmanson.net/boundaries. I recommend reading it because chances are you will learn something about yourself and others in your life. It can help make sense of where your fences are down, then you can decide what you want to do about them.

My advice about boundaries is this:

1. If someone repeatedly causes you pain or tries to make you feel guilty – call them out on it. Ask them to stop!
2. If your generous spirit is taken advantage of ask yourself why you are giving so much. Do you want to be seen as a hero or a martyr?
3. Limit the time you spend with those that try to suck you into their dramas. You can say, "I'm sorry you are having a difficult time at the moment, I hope things improve for you soon!" then walk slowly away, so it does not look like you are running from them.
4. Let people know what is important to you and why! They can't argue with that.
5. State your needs at home and work. Be clear and remind people if they forget.
6. Learn to say yes when you mean yes and no when you mean no! A solid, "No, I can't do that at this time" will not make you look rude or lazy.
7. Notice when others in your life are being taken advantage of and rather than try and fix their situation just learn from the experience.
8. If you are a victim or a saviour – just stop! You are only hurting yourself.
9. Know your motives for doing something. Is it to build your self-esteem or to fuel your ego? If your motives are pure and you expect nothing in return then you will not get hurt.
10. It takes time to practise and set healthy boundaries in all areas of your life, both socially and professionally. Don't be afraid of it, your life will expand when you keep all the wildebeest from roaming around your Serengeti and trampling your defences!

In this step I've encouraged you to expand your social circles, meet new, inspiring and positive people and to help build people up. In helping to build others up, you build yourself up. There is enough of everything for more than one of us to be good at something. You don't need to worry if it looks like someone else is doing the same thing as you, especially if it comes to business, they will attract the customers that are right for them and you will attract the customers that are right for you and you may share some customers. Projecting your positivity towards others, even if you are competing with them for market share, will only put out good vibes which will come back to you at some point.

Remember that socialising is not about meeting your friends at the pub for a drink, although we know this can be fun. Socialising is about investing in relationships, building your support network, engaging in your community, sharing positive emotions and accomplishments and leaving people you meet with a feeling of increase. In doing all of this you will attract an abundance of new experiences, energy, connections and meaning in your life.

Step 9 Recap

1. Find a healthy social circle.

2. Check your boundaries and firm up your fences.

3. Leave your ego at home when you go out.

4. Never stand in a queue if you have no idea what the line is for.

5. Volunteer your time and engage in community events.

"Be the light you want to see in others."
- The Wellness Poet

"Love is the master key to all the issues of society."
- Abhijit Naskar

I AM Connected

I'm joining the dots and crossing my t's,
Staring intently at flowers and trees,
I hear the pitter patter of little feet,
The rhythmic sound of my own heartbeat,
I'm riding my storm,
Acceptance and gratitude the norm,
I feel it, I see it, I don't overthink it,
I feel the connections and I link it,
My intuition guides me,
While intentions shoot out like roots of a tree,
A little at first then totally unpresuming,
Something inside me has started blooming,
In the moment, I see it's not perfect,
But there's no defect,
I'm not seeking perfection,
I'm seeking calm and quiet reflection,
My mind and body are not dejected,
As I become more fully connected,
I'm soaring, the possibilities are endless,
I've got the tools and keys for success,
Sit back and enjoy my progress.

@thewellnesspoet 🅕 🅞 @thewellnesspoet1

STEP 10

Open

When we choose to be open, we allow things to come into our life without judgement and fear. We can let things unfold and not try to control the circumstances. On the other hand, when we are not open, we limit our learning and growth.

Choosing to be open is an important step in embracing what life throws at you with wonder and gratitude. When was the last time you felt or experienced wonder? In times of wonder, we often choose to become stressed at the uncertainty of things and because we may not be in control of the outcome, rather than understanding that we are all on earth to grow and evolve. Humans have the ability to wonder, which other species do not have – use it or lose it!

When I considered what wonder meant to me, a photo of me sitting on a rock holding a huge flower came to my mind, which was taken around four years of age. That photo holds a lot of wonder for me, "The innocence of the child holding a flower". I wanted to feel that wonder again in the world as an adult.

In Step 10, we are practising openness, which includes vulnerability, for the next 30 days.

It will be a challenge and you will need to set the intention and then remind yourself often. Your default will be to put your guard up when talking to people, posting on social media and performing for your friends and family.

Say to yourself:

> *"I am open to fear, I am open to judgement, I am open to support, I am open to challenges, learning and failing."*

I had been manifesting (and working) on this book for only three months before the opportunity to publish it presented itself. I then had to step into this possibility with wonder and be open to both the challenge that comes with finishing a book and the vulnerability of stating out loud that I had a publishing contract for my book!

My ego told me not to tell people to prevent judgement and criticism. My open mind told me that if I really wanted to manifest my book, I needed to tell people about it and be open to judgement. I've learned and practised that judgement only causes the negativity you feel towards others to be projected back onto yourself.

Once I truly started to understand that I could influence my own reality through non-judgement of myself and others I started to be a passionate supporter of anyone and everyone around me. No matter how well or how little I know you, I'm on your team!

And I don't mean that in a superficial way, I'm just generally wishing the best for people and thinking good things about others and not judging them. This positively influences my internal and external state of being.

This is a profound concept when I think about it, and why it's not discussed more widely is beyond me. Too often, we tear others down, backstab and bitch and criticise. But what if we all knew that every time we embrace judgement and criticism of others, we invite judgement and criticism of ourselves.

I know it can be hard sometimes not to moan about our relatives, a colleague who repeatedly let you down, or a boss who wasn't fair. But what if we could all set that aside, knowing that the person we are moaning about is just like us and doing the best they can. If you treat them with compassion and understanding, then you invite compassion and understanding to yourself. It might sound like hard work, but I can tell you that after you practise this concept with those who are the hardest to deal with, it's a breeze for the other people in your life. Overall, your relationships become a lot less stressful.

Being open can make us very vulnerable and many of us may feel immensely uncomfortable with this. Stephen Russell states it best in his quote about vulnerability:

> *"Vulnerability is the only authentic state. Being vulnerable means being open, for wounding, but also for pleasure. Being open to the wounds of life means also being open to the bounty and beauty. Don't mask or deny your vulnerability: It is your greatest asset. Be vulnerable, quake and shake in your boots with it, the new goodness that is coming to you in the form of people, situations and things can only come to you when you are vulnerable i.e. Open."*

During childhood and adolescence, we can also have our 'openness' closed by our parents' fears of judgement. You only need to know Paulo Coelho's life story to understand how parental fears of judgement tried to prevent the most published author on the planet from ever writing a book, because his choice of career was considered insane. Three times his parents sent him to a mental institution for wanting to pursue creativity.

This demonstrates the cruel way we inflict our own judgements on to our children, which can prevent their openness and potential. Since hearing Paulo tell his story of his adolescence spent in a mental asylum because of his parents' fear of judgment, I have become more mindful of the way I speak about others, and my desire to expose my children to opportunities, as opposed to encouraging them to represent my beliefs, and follow in my footsteps, etc.

Paulo also inspired me to get on with telling people about my book, because if you've always wanted to do something and you don't do it, then you can't say you ever did it. I can't say I'm a writer if I've never published a book, a poem, a blog or whatever. To be a writer, I had to actually do it.

Sometimes our openness is beaten out of us by bullies or abusers and it is important to note many abused children turn off their vulnerability as a coping mechanism. Abused children are often very closed off from their emotions, as they receive many mixed messages from abusers. This makes being open and vulnerable as an adult a fairly difficult concept to embrace.

Statistics show that one in five adults suffered sexual abuse as a child and this affects their openness, trust, vulnerability and difficulty feeling feelings and processing emotions. Abuse is not readily discussed by those that endured it due to the guilt that somehow it was probably their fault.

If you have suffered abuse in any form, being open may not be on your initial list of steps to sort out, and I can understand that. I would again direct you back to your growth zone, because the sooner you get into this zone and get out of your comfort zone (which could mean hiding your feelings and your abuse) then the quicker you can progress with your life and open new avenues for fulfilment, including strong new bonds with others.

Abuse victims are not necessarily broken or scared individuals. Many abused children are resilient, hardworking and independent, which are great traits, but also ones which can prevent true openness.

If you've been ridiculed by teachers, family members or bullies during your formative years, your confidence to shine will be very tarnished. Stepping up to be your own hero will be a challenge, as you may always hear that voice of ridicule in your head. Showing up for yourself and becoming your own hero or rock star is a big step, but one worth taking if you want to share your story and help others.

In order to practise being open for 30 days, try these 10 suggestions:

1. Think about the things you are passionate about and give you a buzz inside.
2. Reflect on the things you have done that brought you fulfilment in the past.
3. Come up with all the excuses you can muster not to do something.
4. Come up with a list of all the reasons you should be open to your passions.
5. Consider your relationship with judgement and who you feel would judge you the most and be unsupportive of you. Should you be really open with them?
6. Look for people who are open, passionate and vulnerable and gravitate towards them. This is where you will find your support network.
7. Start to share your ideas, your thoughts and your feelings with a safe audience initially; close friends who are not bitchy or blabby.
8. Engage with content that is aligned with your idea of openness.
9. Look for opportunities to be open with new people and reflect on what happened when you did that.
10. Let the universe know you are open and then sit back and wait in wonder.

I wrote this book to inspire you to be open in your life.

When you decide to be open, some things in your life become less of a priority as you now know what to give your focus and attention to. You also have 10 months of solid practice in the bank now and will know what to let go of. You can't just sit back and wait on the sofa for the door to swing open and a lottery cheque to come waltzing in. You will actually have to take actions, do some leg work, prioritise a few things, plan and get some ideas flowing. Invest in yourself, learn new skills and answer some critics along the way.

Give very little energy to the last of these (critics) and as much energy as you can to all the others. Critics are just fearful allies, and at some stage they will get on board with you. You don't have to explain yourself to them. If Paulo Coelho waited for his parents' blessing to become a writer, he would have used all his energy convincing his biggest critics and closed himself off to so many opportunities including writing his third novel *The Alchemist*, which has been translated to 39 languages and sold 65 million copies.

When my children see that I am open, I hope too that they will be open and can wonder and be innocent. As much as I want to protect them from all forms of physical, mental and emotional harm, I know that I can't do that. Their life journey is their own and all I can do is be supportive, compassionate and non-judgemental. To let them know that life is not a competition and it's only our soul that is valued in the end. Encourage them to have a good soul and to share whatever they have with others.

The openness and wonder in children is such a gift that mindfulness and being present has really taught me to value and look forward to. The journey home from school when I am quiet and my eldest child comes out with her amazing observations are the highlight of my day.

Her: *"Mum, I didn't know we had a washing machine in the car!"*

Me: *"Oh, that's just the washer for the windscreen!"*

Her: *"Oh, I wish I was a car!"*

or

Her: *"Mum, when I grow up, I want to be a Fairy Godmother!"*

Me: *"Oh, that's lovely, why?"*

Her: *"Because then I can make all the other children's wishes come true and bring the dead soldiers back to life!"*

Or

Her: *"Mum, If God made people, who made God? Mum, who is God's Dad?"*

Usually, I'm either crying or laughing and can't come up with an appropriate explanation in that moment, so I just tell her it's a great question and we should ask Dad, the Teacher, Minister, etc....

The wonder and openness of a five-year-old is brilliant, funny and heartwarming and reminds me of that little girl sitting on a rock, holding a flower.

I've still got a lot of parenting to do, and I've still got a lot of growing to do. I do not consider myself an expert at anything, but I know a little about a lot of stuff and I like it that way. In some ways I realise I'm open to stumbling along a bit, making some mistakes and not pretending I know it all, because how can I be open and growing if I think I know everything.

After practising being open for 30 days you will notice some really interesting things:

1. You start to feel clear about your purpose in life.
2. You enjoy small interactions that enable you to connect with someone or something.
3. You have started to attract a whole new bunch of encouraging people who are helping and supporting you.
4. You have let go of some fears and doubts and the internal critic is on holiday.
5. You start to find a flow that was lacking before, things just seem to flow easily.

Step 10 Recap

1. Embrace your vulnerability, it's where the magic happens.

2. Seek wonder in your life.

3. Practise non-judgement of yourself and others.

4. Make a list of your passions and what gives you a buzz.

5. Use your gifts to help others.

"With each passage of human growth, we must shed a protective structure (like a hardy crustacean). We are left exposed and vulnerable – but also yeasty and embryonic again, capable of stretching in ways we hadn't known before."
- Gail Sheehy

"To share your weakness is to make yourself vulnerable; to make yourself vulnerable is to show your strength!"
- Criss Jami

Intuition

When you feel like making a decision,
You can look inside and trust your intuition,
There's a voice inside that is keeping you right,
It provides you with all the wisdom and insight.

So, take the thinking out of your head,
Put your worries, concerns and doubts to bed,
Wake up refreshed with a clear direction,
You can't go wrong when you have the right intention.

The good thing about life, is if we make a mistake,
We have many chances to do a re-take,
You can follow your heart and leave out the head,
Let your intuition guide you instead.

To a place that is kinder and purer and freer,
A place that will bring you nearer,
To all the things you want in your life,
Without all the drama, trouble and strife.

Believe your ability to discover your calling,
Your intuition will stop you from falling,
And if you allow it to keep you right,
The world will give you an abundance of light.

@thewellnesspoet 🅕 🅞 @thewellnesspoet1

STEP 11

New

Congratulations, you are almost there!

Your transformation is close to completion and you are ready to take on new things in your life and look forward to new opportunities, new ideas, new thought patterns, new relationships, new connections, new goals, new resilience, new skills and new freedoms. You will have also created some new neural pathways and developed amazing skills to practise and refine over time. It takes work to keep things fresh in our life and to keep moving forward in a healthy direction.

Too often I hear stories from people about opportunities that are not available to them, because they are competing with someone else or people don't think of them when opportunities come up. If we choose not to evolve and move with the times, keep ourselves relevant and are not brave enough to embrace changes, we will find ourselves left behind in both a professional and a social context.

If you avoid social media, for instance, you will soon become disconnected from life as others around you embrace it for everyday activities like networking, social events, job searching, shopping, learning, etc. If you neglect to update your skills or adapt with the changing needs of businesses, you will be left behind when it comes to being employable.

Both of these elements are important due to the fact that we are all living longer and many of us will need to continue working in our 60s and probably 70s. Not only do we need to be healthy physically, but we need to be up-to-date with modern life. If you are a parent now, the jobs your children will do probably haven't been invented yet. We need to raise creative, resilient children with innovative ideas and an unbreakable spirit. Therefore, it makes sense that we lead by example for our children.

In January 2020, a colleague of mine received an email from a 103-year-old man, sent from his iPad! I had the pleasure of writing the reply to this amazing human and war hero. It was a very emotive experience. Not only had this man done so much for so many, but he was still active, healthy and keeping with the times. A true inspiration for all of us.

In Step 11 we need to continually challenge ourselves to try new things, change our perspective and adopt new ways of doing things.

Now that you are 'Open and Vulnerable' and know how to find your 'Learning and Growth Zone' you can embrace Step 11 with a vengeance. There really is no place for a fixed mindset in the coming decades as we face new challenges in life on this amazing planet.

If you are not familiar with fixed versus growth mindset, you can do some research about it online or read Carol Dweck's book called *Mindset*. It's a useful resource to help you understand your mindset when it comes to work, social situations, learning, parenting and personal growth.

It's natural to want stick with what works for us and to rely on our strengths as we go about our life. In this step we are going to embrace new experiences and opportunities that are going to present themselves, and we are going to be extremely mindful to consider what we need to attract in our life that is going to keep us relevant and engaged for years to come.

For the next 30 days you will review what you have learned about yourself over the previous 300 days, and do some soul searching about your mindset. I ask you to embrace your creativity, explore your thinking on a range of topics and consider new ways of doing things you may have been doing for decades. Demonstrate innovation to yourself and share new ways of doing things with others. Start learning some new skills that may have previously seemed unnecessary, and learn new subjects to have a more informed view of the world around you.

There are a lot of free classes, workshops, seminars, ebooks, documentaries and groups that can assist you learning new stuff. The key thing is to seek and sponge up ideas that you can apply to your life, both now and in the future. Set an example for your family by embracing new ideas and skills that you can start to apply to all areas of your life.

Here's some questions to help understand your mindset:

- Do you learn from your experiences, or repeat the same patterns over and over?
- Have you failed at something and found a way to improve next time?
- Do you blame yourself or others when you make a mistake or fail at a task?
- Do you expect that everyone should think the same way as you?
- Do you dismiss ideas if they are outside of your own belief system?
- Are you happy with the status quo and uncomfortable when things change?
- Have you updated your skills or taken any personal development workshops recently?
- Do you like learning new skills and challenging yourself to try new ways of doing the same task?

If you have a fixed mindset, you are more likely to blame others when you make mistakes or things don't go the way you planned them. A person with a fixed mindset will rely on their natural abilities to try and get by, rather than embrace the opportunity to learn and recognise that mistakes are a part of life.

A person with a growth mindset will generally adopt new ideas and strategies to achieve results, and they will find ways to improve when they make a mistake.

Someone with a fixed mindset can learn to develop a growth mindset if they are willing to consider their weaknesses and learn from their mistakes. It takes practise to embrace a growth mindset, especially if you've lived with a fixed mindset all your life, believing your talents are enough to get you by and your belief systems are quite rigid.

Regardless of how successful you are, academically or in business, you can still have a fixed mindset. Someone with a fixed mindset will eventually come unstuck, because as everything changes around them, they will not change and sooner or later they become redundant.

You only have to look at brands we don't buy or need any more to understand this point. Do you want to be that brand that no-one needs anymore, or do you want to be a forever brand?

Take a look at a company like BP, a brand we all associate with oil, which has over time tried to re-brand and to market itself as a company that provides energy in all its dynamic forms. Had the Gulf of Mexico disaster not occurred they may have achieved their goal much faster, but unfortunately for them they will be forever associated with this horrific oil spill that affected so many lives and livelihoods, not to mention the environmental impact. Oil companies are working hard to try and future-proof their businesses.

Businesses and solo entrepreneurs who adapted quickly to the coronavirus pandemic may have more chance of succeeding and being around after the crisis is over.

For those that don't remember the GFC (Global Financial Crisis) of 2008/9, they were tough years for many of us who lost our jobs. My partner and I ended up taking low-skilled jobs to make ends meet. I cared for a teenager in a wheelchair, while my husband worked in a restaurant. I remember thinking to myself, what can I do to make money to live? What skills do I have that can help me get a job quickly? What do I need to do right now that I can change later if I need to?

It was a quick and dirty assessment of where I was and what I needed to do to survive. But I didn't lose my home and I did not sit around and worry that there was no work. I took immediate action. I was then lucky that I managed to get work in South Africa on the Football World Cup, even though I spent almost five months away from home.

You may need to regularly adopt this mindset and take immediate action. Some good questions to ask yourself are as follows:

- What immediate action can you take now to help yourself?
- What does your dynamic form look like in 10, 20, 30 years from now?
- Are you embracing or resisting change?

Write down 10 new things that you can do to change, grow or innovate in the coming year ahead and then set an intention to start working on them today.

If you are stuck for ideas, here's a few to get you started:

1. Learn to use a new piece of software that will help save you time or look more professional.
2. Take a professional development course.
3. Start a vegetable garden and grow your own food.
4. Start recycling water at home. Empty drink bottles on the garden, use bath water to water the plants, put the washing machine water to the lawn.
5. Learn how to cook using different ingredients from a variety of sources.
6. Shop at the farmer's market instead of the supermarket and talk to the people who grow your food.
7. Take public transport whenever you can.
8. Adopt solar energy wherever possible.
9. Share food with neighbours and friends rather than throw it away.

10. Recycle and repurpose everyday items to avoid them going to landfill.
11. Write your autobiography for your children.
12. Take art or photography classes.
13. Visit different places regularly to meet new people and expose yourself to new ideas.
14. Plant native trees and shrubs around your home.
15. Volunteer your time to help others learn and grow.
16. Switch off the TV and spend time in nature as much as possible.
17. Spend time with the elderly asking them what they thought of the world when they were your age.
18. Read books aimed at growth and personal development.
19. Ask questions, research and be curious about topics that you aren't quite sure about, or have no knowledge of.
20. Talk to your children about the kind of future they see and ask them what they would like to learn and do it with them.

Think about the key things you need to do now that will future proof you personally, professionally and physically.

Taking a new direction in life or adding new skills and experiences doesn't just happen by chance, it takes some effort and consideration. However, once the intention is set and the actions toward them unfold, they will happen more effortlessly than if you try to force change too quickly by stopping and starting something new every time you get stuck. It can be natural to want to give up on something very quickly when we find it's not working. Perseverance and adaptability are not skills we boast about on our CV, but they are so important for navigating challenges when things come up that seem hard. Rather than give up, we can find a way through by seeing a new solution to an old problem, this is called innovation.

In 2019, Oprah interviewed Shaka Senghor who wrote a book called *Writing My Wrongs: Life, Death, and Redemption in an American Prison*. He talks about innovation and resilience and forgiveness. His story is sad and frightening, but the power of his story is transformative. After 20 years in prison, he gets out and it is a whole new world, but he is able to draw on his prison experience to overcome all his obstacles and earn a Fellowship from MIT, win Innovator of the Year from Manchester University and write a New York Times best-selling memoir.

What Shaka's story teaches all of us is that if he can, we can. If someone who was in prison for murder can grow, thrive, learn, create, innovate and help others, then we all can. We have no excuses. The only thing holding us back is our beliefs and our mindset.

The next 5–10 years are critical for life on this planet, and it will take brave new thinking to start to undo the damage we have caused to the environment and to our own health. The quicker we start to understand that we need to prioritise the health of ourselves and our environment, the better life will be for ourselves and our children. Taking our life and the world around us for granted has really been a detrimental way of living for so many of us.

Outsourcing our health and wellness, outsourcing our happiness and outsourcing our lives to others means we lack the accountability to make changes in our internal world and our external world.

Hopefully in the previous 10 Steps you've come to understand this and are ready to embrace a new mindset about yourself, as well as your surroundings. If you've already clocked this and started to embrace changes and innovation, then well done, keep going, be a beacon for others. I don't expect perfection of you or myself, I hope for sustained and continued effort and willingness to try and do the right thing.

I would like to mention that embracing new does not necessarily mean spending money on all new things and new gadgets. We need to be mindful of appreciating what we have, practising sufficiency, but at the same time knowing that change and innovation is inevitable. We need to do it in a sustainable way.

Your idea of "new" and "growth" will be different from the next person and that's okay. We all contribute in our own way, but like I said earlier, if our intentions are good and we are not deliberately trying to hurt others then there are no bad ideas, it's all part of the process.

Take time to share new experiences with others and take time to ask your loved ones what new things they learnt or heard this week. It may just spark a whole raft of ideas and possibilities. Listening to the same stuff every day is only going to reinforce the same beliefs and views. Make a change, expose your mind to new ideas and be accountable for your learning and growth. Let your spirit roam free, with endless possibilities and wisdom.

In this step you will broaden your mind and let your spirit guide you towards a new life. Keep this practice ongoing for continual learning, growth, development and self-actualisation.

My Spirit

I sit here watching day by day,
My life before me pass away,
And even though no-one else can see,
At least I know my spirit's free.

@thewellnesspoet 　　 @thewellnesspoet1

Step 11 Recap

1. Start to understand your default mindset: fixed or growth.

2. Look for new ways to innovate and share your passions.

3. Be a positive role model for your family by embracing change and being responsive to challenges.

4. Learn new skills and share your skills with others.

5. Recognise if you are stagnating or innovating and keep growing.

"The definition of insanity is doing the same thing over and over and expecting a different result."

\- Albert Einstein

"Your life does not get better by chance, it gets better by change."

– Jim Rohn

Uncertainty

I'm getting comfortable with the uncomfortable,
I've lost the fear in the here,
And I'm starting to feel the wow, in the now!
It's getting easier to sense the anxiety and enjoy a new sobriety.

There's space within each place that allows me to think
and grow,
Without the limits and the self-doubt, I used to know.
There's more beauty in the future, where my heart is clear
and pure,
My mind can't hold me back, it's not something to endure.

I have a sense of wonder about each and every moment,
I breathe away the cloud of thought stopping my enlightenment,
My eyes are wide open, my breathing has meaning,
My body is responding with energy and feeling.

The uncertainty is lifting, I can stop my mind drifting,
To the fear and doubts, the worries and bouts,
That before were my normal, and now quite uncalled for.

Uncertainty is a friend, in whose presence I like to spend,
My time with this friend is not at the beginning or at the end,
An ongoing and wondrous place to enjoy and embrace,
There's no uncertainty to erase.

@thewellnesspoet @thewellnesspoet1

STEP 12

Devoted

Devoted has become a word we associate with those we love. Throughout this book I have sought to encourage you to prioritise your own self-love.

If you've been following all the steps in this book and have reached Step 12, you are now ready to test your devotion to self-love and all the new healthy habits you have acquired, and to do that you may need to test your new skills in a different environment to see how they hold up under differing circumstances.

In Step 12 we will consider how being devoted to self-love, self-care and self-acceptance are three keys that unlock your hidden potential and we will practise this devotion.

It's quite easy to maintain a good routine and have daily practice in health, wellbeing, exercise, mindfulness, compassion, joy, meditation and journaling, but when you hit a busy period, a stressful period, a life change, Christmas holidays with extended family... how the heck to do you stop the carefully woven web from being swept aside and left in tatters?

You do know that at some stage you are going to potentially experience a change in routine or to your personal circumstances. So, what can you do to protect your good habits?

Here's what I recommend:

1. Remember what your bad habits were and how you developed them.
2. Think about the future situations you may find yourself in and the decisions you will have to make.
3. Challenge yourself to make healthy choices daily.
4. Plan to spend time doing all of the previous 11 Steps regularly during any holidays or transition periods.
5. Hold yourself accountable for your health and share your experiences with others.

6. Find new ways to practise health and wellbeing. Try something new!

7. Connect with others nearby who you can buddy up with to walk, talk, write or laugh.

8. If you are travelling abroad, write a healthy to-do list for your travels, which could include:

    a. Pack supplements for each day.

    b. Stretch before, during and after each flight and daily during the time away.

    c. Choose healthy meal options where ever possible, especially during long-haul flights.

    d. Limit the days when you know you may consume alcohol.

    e. Plan time to exercise, even just 30 minutes.

    f. Spend time with people who are supportive and kind.

    g. Get as much rest as you can.

    h. Choose a daily meditation that fits in with your routine and commit to doing it, even if it's on a crowded plane or train.

    i. Drink lots of water.

    j. Appreciate the opportunities you have so when things feel stressful or tiresome you don't start feeling sorry for yourself.

You will have setbacks and there will be days when you just want to drink lots of wine and eat lots of chocolate. Enjoy it and forgive yourself. You've done the work, you can relax in the knowledge that you have all the tools to pick up where you left off and start again.

No-one is perfect and we all have challenging moments in life after working long hours, sleepless nights, pain, emotional hurdles, difficult co-workers or worries for our family. We can drive ourselves insane if we let all of these build up day after day, so it's important to acknowledge them as soon as you practically can and address them, before they become much bigger longer-term issues. The sooner you embrace a challenge, own it and recognise that it might cause you anxiety, the quicker you can find the right solution or let it go.

Inside each of us we have a vault of stories and potential. Our stories shape us and may define our potential. These stories also have the ability to block our potential when we get stuck in a story and loop it over and over, both mentally and in reality.

Being devoted to yourself does not mean that you put yourself above all others. It purely means that you are devoted to looking after yourself and ensuring you give yourself the best chance of health, happiness, wellbeing and success in whatever form that takes for you.

We are all dealt some pretty big blows in life and they can come at any time. You may not have all the skills and tools needed to cope or to manage the situation and you may feel utterly broken.

What's amazing in our relatively safe, modern society is that there is help all around us. Information, support, medical treatment, forums, etc. There is literally any number of avenues for help, available to a very large percentage of our population. So, if you repeatedly find yourself broken, stressed, stuck, or ill, you have ample avenues to break that cycle.

The cycle that is most difficult to break is our internal dialogue. It tells us what we can, and cannot do, and makes us worry, stress, self-sabotage, self-abuse and self-criticise. Who wants to be devoted to that?

Strangely, a large percentage of us are. We are devoted to stress and self-abuse through neglect of our health and wellbeing and devoted to being unhappy by thinking and thinking and thinking and just not being.

"Being present, being kind, being peaceful, being compassionate and being helpful."

True happiness and fulfilment come from being content with who we are and what we have, regardless of how little, or how much.

The test of how devoted I was to myself and the steps in this book came during December when it's normal to travel, visit family and see friends. Typically, in Australia our children are also on holidays for two months, which is a challenge in itself for most working parents.

My employer offered me the opportunity to travel to the UK for two weeks in December to deliver some training sessions and meet with our clients and I decided to take my eldest daughter with me. She is generally a good flyer, so I wasn't worried about the travel, but there had been a terrorist attack in the week before our trip. I was conscious of booking accommodation that was safe and to ensure our days were planned well so as to avoid too much time waiting around or sitting on public transport during rush hour.

I packed my supplements, running gear and our winter clothes. I made a rough plan of when I could exercise, considered where and when I would buy and eat healthy food (knowing there would be some special treats). I put together a detailed itinerary so I could work and we could spend time with those we loved and my daughter could see all my husband's extended family.

Overall, the trip was a huge success for both my daughter and I, and largely I did not feel stressed or overwhelmed even once. My eating, exercise and stretching routine worked a treat to combat jet lag and acclimatise from Summer to Winter as quickly as possible.

On the return journey from London which is a 24-hour marathon, I was tested at the airport. We'd been up since 4am to get there on time and I've learned two things travelling long-haul with small children: you will either fly through the airport receiving nothing but goodwill from people; or you will encounter delay after delay and end up being messed around, exhausted and totally stressed and sweaty before a long-haul flight, which is no way to embark on your journey.

I always aim for version one of this scenario, determined not to be sweaty and stressed and allow a lot of time for extra baggage checks, toilet stops, family queues (which are a freaking nightmare thank you very much!) and time to grab the last-minute presents.

I travelled a lot with my daughter when she was a baby, so I always tend to overpack my hand luggage knowing that it's better to have too many clothes and back up food for all eventualities. My airport experiences over the years could fill a whole other book.

I'd also had a funny tummy for a few days leading up to the flight (after trying some new foods) and my daughter was very tired and quite grumpy from being woken at 4am. Check-in was smooth and we relaxed in a café for breakfast before our first 13-hour flight. We then had a 15-minute walk to get to our departure gate (four pieces of hand luggage, a small tired child and a 15-minute walk before the 24-hour journey – deep breaths required here!). It was not a movie star airport walk!

At the departure gate, my tummy told me I urgently needed to go to the toilet. I quickly gathered up our four pieces of hand luggage to find the nearest loo, and by this time my five-year-old, was really starting to have a wobbly (tantrum) and my knees were starting to get very wobbly. I could feel myself getting frustrated, and about to lose my 'you know what' with her, as I was doing, 'you know what'!

I gave her my sternest voice, *"At this moment, I can't help you, because Mummy is doing a poopoo, so please hold it together, and when I've finished, we can talk about this, okay?"*

Through her sobs she agreed to try and hold it together, while I mindfully checked in with myself to see if my reaction was appropriate given the circumstances and to acknowledge how I was feeling, and to be compassionate to how she must be feeling. In those 15 seconds of mindfulness, I decided to cut myself some slack, I was doing the best I could, we were both safe and I loved her. As soon as I was out of that crappy crapper, I would give her some Mumma lovin'.

And that's what we did. We found a quiet corner, had lots of hugs, laughs and did some yoga, and boarded our flight together as two loving friends. I have to say, this was quite a moment for me. After getting up at 4am and during the following five hours dealing with the rain, the cold, the luggage, the child, my own human needs and thousands of other people in similar circumstances, I did not allow myself to become stressed, to feel sorry for myself, to blame others for how I was feeling and not take care of my mind and body.

And here's the other thing; I recognise that these are First World problems. I'm privileged to have this opportunity. I don't need to create drama out of First World problems and get caught up in silly dramas. In the same way, I don't need to create drama and stress about other privileges we have, such as our children's birthday parties, buying a house, doing our taxes, getting repairs to our house, going to work each day. If something is seriously causing you stress and anguish, in most instances you have the opportunity to stop it, change it, or accept it.

It was a 100% success story. I'm not perfect, but I do feel like I was perfectly devoted to my new habits, my rituals, my wellbeing, my running, my writing and my lifestyle – and that's a massive accomplishment. I was able to travel to the other side of the world for two weeks with a five-year-old and follow all 12 Steps whilst working, cooking, washing and changing hotels five times in two weeks.

I incorporated all 12 Steps into my working holiday routine and I was able to:

1. Meet clients and fulfil my working commitments.
2. Write in my journal and four chapters of this book.
3. File my tax return.
4. Be mindful of my thoughts and feelings and notice what was coming up for me and why it was important.
5. Appreciate all the people in the world that care about us, welcomed us and took care of us during the trip and over the holiday season.

6. Meditate.
7. Notice moments of sheer joy with my daughter and in nature (even when it was freezing cold).
8. Jog in cold and wet places and enjoy the thrill of it (when I had someone to stay with my daughter).
9. Seek adventure in doing things we had not done before, which included embarking on this journey that took me away from home and my youngest child, whilst allowing my eldest to experience some incredible moments and see her extended family.
10. Be sociable as much as practically possible with a child in tow, and to balance her need for social engagements with my own. I swear she had more socialising and adventures than I did.
11. Open myself up to people, to share my experiences, my new knowledge and the idea for this book, and to ask for help and support from others.
12. Buy some new clothes to fit my much smaller frame and lay some new foundations for my future.

In setting out these 12 Steps and practising them for 30 days, one after the other and also in parallel, I transformed not just my health but my future. I can't wait to see what comes next. I can't wait to see where my next opportunity comes from, because opportunities are abundant for all of us, and taking a chance to speak to someone nearby you could open up the next most exciting chapter of your life. Now I feel hopelessly devoted to this approach to living, my foundations are complete.

The thing about these 12 Steps is that you don't just do them once and then go back to how things were before you picked up your first journal. You keep going, you keep the intentions and practise them as part of your everyday life. By keeping the 12 Steps going in unison it's going to keep propelling you in the right direction, and you may find more energy to take on new challenges, to continue the expansion in your growth zone, to learn new skills and experience new people in your life.

It's entirely feasible that at the end of these 12 Steps you will feel so great that you feel unbreakable. Of course, you may have moments of self-doubt, and meet people who are not supportive and face things you can't control. However, you now have the tools that even if these things do occur, you can review them, acknowledge them and see them for what they are.

It could be your ego needs a check-up and that when you worry about failing, it's just your ego trying to stop you from growing and learning. It wants to keep you safe. Look into your soul and ask it how you are doing? If you are doing things to nourish your soul and to help others, your doubts will be short-lived.

Yes, it's a vulnerable time. You are about to step out and say, *"Hey, look at me, I am enough, I am kind, I am free, I am me"*. And some people won't like that. That's cool, we are just all making our own way on this planet and you can only be a role model to yourself first and foremost. The best leaders on the planet are the most compassionate people. So be a leader, be compassionate, role model your values, role model your behaviours and role model how you want to be treated.

If you are looking for things to be devoted to, you may have overlooked the key principle of this book: you need to be devoted to you.

For the next 30 days, I want you to look in the mirror and say to yourself:

"Thank you for all that you have done for me, I am devoted to you."

"I will take care of you."

"I will ensure your needs are met and that you feel loved and cared for."

"I am devoted to your success and your unbreakable spirit."

At the end of 360 days, I hope you are not only devoted to yourself, but that you inspire others to be devoted to themselves. In finding meaning, purpose, joy and love for yourself, you are giving everyone else permission to be devoted to you. Step to the front and centre and be connected to whatever and whoever you feel is vibrating at the same frequency as you.

"Your vibe attracts your tribe, your unity builds your community. Go out and spread your devotion far and wide."

Step 12 Recap

1. Devotion starts with yourself.

2. Practise devotion to these 12 Steps ongoing and in parallel.

3. Be a leader and role model your values and behaviours.

4. Be present, be kind, be peaceful, be compassionate and be helpful.

5. Recognise your opportunities and your gifts and count your blessings.

"It is under the greatest adversity that there exists the greatest potential for doing good, both for oneself and others."

- Dalai Lama

"To improve is to change, to be perfect is to change often".

- Winston Churchill

Serenity

A peaceful moment, untroubled by torment,
A calm sensation, not a hint of frustration,
Perhaps it's the place or a smile on the face,
An inner quiet, a feeling of delight,
Opportunities are abundant, fear is redundant,
Hope and wonder are normal, it's written in your journal,
Kindness and grace leave a legacy that cannot be replaced,
It's your life to shape and yours to create, it's never too late,
It's in the eye of the beholder and it's in the heart of the moulder,
Serenity comes with no penalty, it's not bought with prosperity,
It will bring longevity in your soul for eternity.

@thewellnesspoet 〔f〕 〔o〕 @thewellnesspoet1

12 Months from Broken to Unbreakable!

@thewellnesspoet1 @thewellnesspoet1

Afterword

The intention for this book was to share relevant stories that you could relate to. In practising these 12 Steps, you too have the ability to see through your experiences, beliefs and challenges.

When you become fully accountable for how you show up in your life for yourself and others, you realise that everything you think, and every experience you have, is down to you. Dr Joe Dispenza teaches us that, "Your personality defines your personal reality and your personal reality defines your personality!"

Our personality is not inherited, it's not in our DNA. Our personal reality is not inherited or set in stone. Excuses, fears, judgement, stress, expectations, worries, anxiety and limiting beliefs dictate how we live our lives. When you fully embrace those facts and take accountability for your thoughts, actions, hopes and fears, then you will start to live a much healthier balanced life.

You will know when things become too much for you and you will take a step back. You will know when things feel right and you will jump in. You will know when your body needs rest or when your thoughts are becoming unhelpful and you can remind yourself to go back to being grateful with your life and all the opportunities that are available to you, if you have allowed yourself to see them.

To get the best out of this book, you may like to read it cover to cover and then set your intention to follow each step for 30 days. If you choose to start in January, then you know by December you will be totally devoted to a new way of living, and like me, you will be fitter, healthier, happier and more connected. However, do not wait for January, you can start today. Grab your journal and just note down the date you started and every 30 days move on to the next step.

I'm conscious that at the time of finalising this book, we are in the early stages of the coronavirus pandemic and the long-term implications of this may not be understood for a very long time. Many people will suffer physically and financially and I pray for everyone affected.

I call myself a Wellness Warrior, wanting to spread a message of health and wellness like a virus. I still believe that we can do this and help minimise the impact of illness and diseases. Taking accountability for our own health is the first step.

You will probably have clocked that throughout this book I do not mention my partner very often. That is because this journey is my own and the story in this book is my own story, not his. Over 17 years I have been a good wife and a good partner, however even those closest to us often can't influence what we think and feel: it's up to us. They can support us, help us and love us but still our journey is our own, only we can make ourselves unbreakable.

Good luck with your journey from Broken to Unbreakable.

Remember, I'm on your team and you can contact me anytime for help, support or encouragement.

Krissy Regan, The Wellness Poet

thewellnesspoet@gmail.com

Top 20 Tips for an Unbreakable Mind, Body and Spirit

1. Prioritise your sleep and set a good bedtime routine.
2. Complete 3 x 25 minutes of vigorous exercise per week.
3. Meditate 10-12 minutes each day.
4. Say a gratitude prayer each evening before bed, acknowledge all you are thankful for that day and in your life.
5. Compliment others sincerely and as much as you can.
6. Leave everyone you meet with a feeling of increase because they came in contact with you.
7. Stretch daily for 30-40 minutes.
8. Write in your journal regularly - it's the unspoken words in your soul.
9. Avoid saying and thinking negative things about people, as you only attract negativity towards yourself.
10. Spend time in nature and allow your energy to connect with the world around you.
11. Notice bird song, flower blooms and the breeze on your skin.
12. Notice moments of joy and acknowledge the impact in your heart and soul.
13. Step outside your comfort zone on a regular basis.
14. Try new things regularly and talk about them.
15. Laugh and hug as much as you can.
16. Forgive yourself and others in order to grow and heal.
17. Share your love and passion with others.
18. Take time out for self-care, self-love, self-acceptance and self-improvement.
19. Take accountability for your own health and educate yourself about food and nutrition so you can make good choices and remember, food is the best medicine.
20. Eat as many whole plant-based foods as you can and limit consumption of animal based products in your diet which can cause inflammation and disease.

Walk with Me!

Each month I **GIVE AWAY** two free, 30-minute 'Walk and Talks' in which we talk about the contents of the book relative to your life and how it can best help you. Regardless of where you live, I connect with you on any platform, in any time zone and we walk and talk together, sharing stories, insights and support. Email me for further details and availability:
thewellnesspoet@gmail.com

@thewellnesspoet 🅵 🅾 @thewellnesspoet1

Join our
Unbreakable Community
on Facebook!

Once you have read the book please contact
Krissy Regan, The Wellness Poet via email or messenger and
request to join the **Closed Facebook Members Group,**
"The Unbreakable Community".

In this Group you will have access to:

- **Weekly Live Chats and Q&A's with Krissy**
- **Access to exclusive video content via secret YouTube videos**
- **Hints, Tips and Downloads**
- **Access to Online Courses**
- **VIP Access for Book Signings, Seminars and Programs**
- **A Discount Code for Products and Services purchased via Krissy's website or via direct invoice**
- **Exclusive Pre-orders for Krissy's annual combined Wellness Planner and Journal**

www.thewellnesspoet.com
thewellnesspoet@gmail.com
or message @thewellnesspoet

@thewellnesspoet  @thewellnesspoet1

Krissy Regan is an Author, Poet, International Speaker and Health & Wellness Coach, and is passionate about helping people feel their best at work and home. She has worked and competed on the international stage for the past 20 years, after stepping on to the world's biggest stage as a performer in the Opening Ceremony of the Sydney Olympics.

Since attaining an Exercise Science and Sports Management Degree she has travelled to more than 40 countries and lived in seven. Her love of sport and project management ensured her success, working on many global sporting events, helping brands deliver life changing moments for their clients. After decades of travelling and managing her clients' projects, she decided it was time to pursue her own goal; to write a book, share her experiences to serve others and craft a blueprint which enables working parents to balance working life with family life.

Krissy founded Mindful Mums Queensland in 2019 and offers empowerment and mindfulness programs for a global community of mums. She is also an Executive Board Member of Queensland Youth Services.

Krissy has developed and delivered training programs all over the world, and has even been lucky enough to train staff at Buckingham Palace. Krissy's skill as a coach comes from her ability to break down tasks and ideas into manageable steps and create compelling content from technical information.

Typical Speaking Topics Include:

Mindfulness and Thinking Interventions (Wellbeing is not a Dirty Word)
- Understanding Stress and Stress Management at Home and Work.
- Employee Thinking Interventions for Managing Stress.
- How to wake up every day with a spring in your step (organisational tips for busy working parents).

Healthy Staff, Healthy Profits
- The Secret Investment to your Business Success.
- Embracing the Wellness Movement at Work.
- Creating a Healthy Environment in your Workplace.

Leadership for Modern Life
- Creating more Mindful Leaders in the Workplace.
- Increase Staff Retention Long Term.
- Balancing the Demands of Home vs Office Working.

BOOK Krissy for your next event, conference or company webinar.
EMAIL: thewellnesspoet@gmail.com

"Krissy, I don't know how you do it. You are the Maestro of Staff Training #justsayin'. Having seen you in action in Warsaw, Rio, Tokyo and London, I'm always amazed at what you can deliver!"
Juliette Schmidt, Berlin, Germany.

"Krissy combines a wealth of experience in leadership, project management, client handling and team development. Her training programs are unique, due to her ability to translate complex messages in an engaging, fun and memorable way. Krissy has created bespoke training programs for both our internal and external clients for the past three years and it's always a pleasure to attend her sessions."
Yael Cole-Slagter, Director of Operations, SQR group, London.

"Krissy is a force of nature, with a unique ability to transform ideas into reality despite huge challenges. This book captures the journey of a high-performing working mother, through Krissy's immense personal experience from home to some of the world's biggest events. An inspirational read for women of the world."

Amy Kemp, New York, USA

"Krissy, I don't know how you do it. You are the Maestro of Staff Training #justsayin'. Having seen you in action in Warsaw, Rio, Tokyo and London, I'm always amazed at what you can deliver!"

Juliette Schmidt, Berlin, Germany

"Krissy has been designing training programs for my client for the past four years. She never ceases to amaze me with her ideas, content, energy and her delivery, which is fun and communicates our client's message in such an informed and inspiring way. I have no hesitation in recommending Krissy to any of my clients!"

Marleen Braams,
Founder, Xselling Events, Brussels, Belgium

"When Krissy told me she was writing this book, I was not surprised. Her ability to communicate complex messages in a simple yet engaging way using her own experiences is both refreshing and inspiring. I can't wait to share the book with my friends!"

Steve McDade, Noosa, Australia

"Good God woman – you really are something! I'm sure that they could use your help at CERN or the International Space Station if you have a moment to spare. Bloody impressed, as ever, that you can find time to write a book, raise kids and work at the same time. You taught me so much about working in a large team and managing remote teams. Having seen you train hundreds of people over the years, I know that this book will make an impact on so many people!"

Cathy Joyce, Vancouver, Canada

"When we decided to introduce a monthly company newsletter to inspire and motivate our staff based all over the world, we asked Krissy to take the lead on this task. Not only is the newsletter inspiring and informative, it helps our remote teams to feel connected to Head Office. Krissy incorporates a wellness section in each newsletter to encourage and motivate staff to take ownership for their health and wellbeing. We look forward to her hints and tips each month and staff have commented about the value this adds to them personally. I can't wait to share her book with our employees!"

Shai Slagter, CEO, SQR group, London

Image Credits

Front Cover Istock.com/Xesai

Introduction Istock.com/SilviaSaez

Step 1 Istock.com/Ekaterina Beklemysheva

Step 2 Istock.com/Rassco

Step 3 Istock.com/MariaStavreva

Step 4 Istock.com/annatodica

Step 5 Istock.com/askmenow

Step 6 Istock.com/AnnaErastova

Step 7 Istock.com/pijama61

Step 8 Istock.com/LianaMonicaBordei

Step 9 Istock.com/VictoriaBar

Step 10 Istock.com/ erhui1979

Step 11 Istock.com/invincible_bulldog

Step 12 Istock.com/erhui1979

Back cover photo Photographer Felicity Cole - Flickaphotography

Notes